Gardening on Clay

Peter Jones

'Valentine Heart' roses.

Gardening on Clay

Peter Jones

THE CROWOOD PRESS

First published in 2009 by
The Crowood Press Ltd
Ramsbury, Marlborough
Wiltshire SN8 2HR

www.crowood.com

British Library Cataloguing-in-Publication Data
A catalogue record for this book is available from the British Library.

ISBN 978 1 84797 081 7

Acknowledgements
The author wishes to thank Peter Lyons of Peter Lyons Books, Cheltenham for his encouragement and enthusiastic support; Pamela Lewis for all her help; David Austin® Roses for their guidance on selecting the best varieties of roses to grow on clay and especially Michael Marriott.

Illustrations by Caroline Pratt
Photographs by Sue Atkinson, David Austin® Roses, Peter Jones, J. Lockwood, Ian Murray and Y. Rees

Typeset by Simon Loxley
Printed and bound in Singapore by Craft Print International

Contents

Introduction

On initial inspection a slice of clay soil can look uninteresting. In the winter it is cold, wet and slimy, almost like plasticine to the touch, varying in colour between shades of brown, yellow and blue. In the summer it has a hard crust, with cracks in places and deep open seams going downwards for one and a half feet (about half a metre) or more. However, with correct cultivation and ongoing management, clay soil can be transformed into one of the most responsive soil types.

Soil that can retain moisture, yet is also able to get rid of surplus moisture to allow air to circulate freely around the soil particles, is the ideal growing medium – and clay soil is certainly not in this category. In the winter it can become sodden, causing plants to drown, particularly if the winter is a cold one. Occasional glimpses of the sun through leaden skies are insufficient to assist drying out, thus it is slow to warm up in the spring and plants are hesitant to grow. But in spite of this, clay is often remarkably fertile, so when the gardener has started to break down the gluey texture, it is often surprising how plants do catch up with others that are growing in more favourable soil.

With the probability of climate change affecting our way of life more each year, we will reach the situation where we will want to use our garden more in the winter months than previously. The type of planting will change, as there will be a greater emphasis on plants and bulbs that flower between November and February, and the introduction to our gardens of plants from areas such as the Mediterranean, which previously we would have considered to be foolhardy. But in order for this to happen we will have to ensure that the growing must be right to support this change: there is no point in having increased above-ground tempera-

tures if the growing conditions below ground level are not able to support this. How to achieve these conditions will be dealt with in this book.

It may be that we will have to introduce natural or man-made shelter screens, because although the temperature may be rising, we will still need these shelters to protect us and the plants from prevailing winds if we want to sit out amongst them – yet another change in design we may have to consider.

Whatever we choose to do and whatever direction we decide to go down, at the end of the day it is the soil that controls what we can and cannot do. The purpose of *Gardening on Clay* is to help you achieve what you want from your garden.

CHAPTER 1

Cultivation

WHERE IS CLAY FOUND?

Clay can be found in the British Isles below a line drawn from the emergence of the River Severn and the River Humber. This is not to say that clay does not appear in isolated pockets elsewhere, for instance in the limey Cotswolds, where occasional acidic pockets give rise to gardens that are different from the normal plantings in the area. Thus you would not expect to find rhododendrons, azaleas and camellias thriving in the Cotswolds, but they do. The intensely clay areas are the Potteries, Birmingham, London, Essex and Kent. These clay-rich areas were the centres of brick-making and domestic ware in the Victorian era of industrial activity.

Breaking down and improving clay soil may require one or more of the following processes:

- Drainage
- Management
- Feeding
- Mulching
- Raised beds

DRAINING THE SOIL

Very waterlogged clay may require artificial drainage – the installation of sloping pipes laid in a herring-bone fashion, some 2ft (60cm) below the surface of the soil. The main artery (backbone) carries the water either to a gravel-filled soakaway or, if you are fortunate to have one in your garden, a ditch or stream. If no outlet is available you may have to install a central soakaway into which each of

With careful management, drainage and feeding, the clay garden can be highly successful.

the herringbones enters. The soakaway must be filled with gravel, to which copious quantities of charcoal are incorporated; this process will prevent the area becoming sour.

If the above is the chosen method, remember where the soakaway is situated and do not introduce plants with an invasive root system here: such plants will find the moisture and clog up the system in a short space of time.

If the drainage of your clay garden does not require such drastic treatment as described above, it is possible that all that is needed is the incorporation of gravel or grit when the ground is cultivated prior to planting or sowing. If the ground is being cultivated by hand, then generous handfuls of gravel or grit can be incorporated as each spadeful is turned over. If an area is to be rotavated, the ground should be covered with the gravel or grit before the machine starts to turn it over.

If at the end of the growing season it is obvious that at times the ground still becomes waterlogged, the above process can be repeated without harm to the soil. Similarly, where plants are in permanent positions, handfuls of gravel can be worked in at their base and surrounding areas using a hand fork without damaging their root structure.

Sometimes it is beneficial at planting time for semi or permanent plants to incorporate some drainage material at the base of the planting hole and around its sides once the plant is *in situ* before filling in the rest of the hole with soil compost. Gravel or grit is excellent for this purpose.

A MANAGEMENT PROGRAMME

Obviously whatever type of soil you have, there must be an annual management programme; this

Fig 1. Mulch spread under a plant two to three inches deep will help suppress weeds.

should not be tucked away in a gardening book or in a drawer, but should be kept in the potting shed or somewhere clearly visible. So that no procedure is forgotten or delayed, a weekly diary with spaces for each day would be ideal.

With clay soil not being the easiest to garden on, it is very important for its wellbeing that such a programme is carried out at the correct time of the growing season. It should list the feeding, mulching, pruning and spraying times, and the instructions for carrying out these procedures. Ideally this job can be carried out after the Christmas festive season is over and when the new diaries are ready to go up, and possibly the weather outside is not inviting to garden in. Once you have started this procedure, remember to keep the previous year's programme, because not only is this a standby should you lose the current one, but it is also a useful record of what has happened in the garden in the previous year or years.

FEEDING YOUR CLAY GARDEN

If the soil is in good heart it may only require an annual feed, preferably in the autumn or winter. This could be a dressing of combined sterilized fish, blood and bone at the rate of 2oz (57g) per square yard or metre. The reason for using sterilized feed is that it loses its smell in the sterilizing process and therefore domestic animals are not tempted to eat it.

Added to the fish, blood and bone should be an application of pelleted chicken fertilizer at the rate of a handful per square yard or metre. This is now readily available in garden centres or horticultural suppliers, and is very economic to use. These feeds should be applied to permanently planted areas as well as vacant areas; it is particularly useful to apply them to the base of walls that have plants trained to go up them, and also to confined planted beds that seldom receive any further feeding after their initial feeding at planting time. Their response is remarkable.

Once the feeds have been applied, it is beneficial to cover the feed with a surface mulch (see below), although this is not always practical in densely planted areas.

Foliar Feeding

Apart from surface feeding, foliar feeding should also be considered. Foliar feeding is much more widely practised in other countries than in Great Britain, but its use is becoming better known over here through the medium of television and the press. It is used during the optimum growing period – from the beginning of May to the end of July – and it is an application of a feed to the foliage of the plant rather than to its roots.

It is applied at a maximum of every two weeks during this period, and is sprayed on to the leaves in the cool of the morning or the evening (but not in the heat of midday, as this would cause scorching to the leaves). It consists of an application of concentrated seaweed fertilizer that has a high trace-element content. Maxicrop and Seagold are two of the best brands available. The application rate is one tablespoonful of the feed to a gallon of water, to which five or six drops of washing-up liquid have been added and thoroughly stirred in. The washing-up liquid acts as a fixative, ensuring that the feed is thoroughly absorbed by the plant and is not washed off in the first shower of rain. It is beneficial to all growing plants, whether trees, shrubs, perennials, annuals, vegetables or fruit. It promotes healthy growth that in turn helps plants to combat attacks from pests and diseases.

MULCHING

With the advent of climate change, the application of a surface mulch to the soil is imperative. Mulching is an application of a covering material to prevent the sun in the growing season from drying out the moisture that has fallen over the winter months.

Ideally a mulch should be applied in either February or March, when the winter rains have penetrated deeply into the soil. The other benefit of

---

CREATING YOUR OWN COMPOST HEAP

Whatever type of soil you have, every garden should have a compost heap. They cost nothing to make once you have the container; in fact, some local authorities actually provide these free of charge.

Where people go wrong is to make the heap too large. Ideally it should not exceed 4 x 4 x 4ft (1.2m). It can have a base, or be situated directly on the surface of the soil, and it should have solid sides and a movable top. As soon as the first waste material is placed into the container, it should be covered with a sheet of black plastic as this generates heat, which leads to the subsequent decay of the materials. Every time more material is added, ensure the plastic is replaced. All vegetable matter will decay under these conditions – orange, grapefruit, banana skins can all be put in, and if you can get the heap really hot, weeds as well as household waste can be used. You can purchase a compost activator to hasten the process, but if human urine is added on a regular basis this is just as good, if not better, and is free!

When the container is full, allow it to stand for two to three months, and at the end of this time, out should come a dark, crumbly material ready to be worked into the soil or applied as a surface mulch. Leaves can be rotted down in the same way to supply you with leaf mould, as can grass, though before you mow, place a layer of crumpled up newspaper on the previous layer, otherwise the grass takes ages to decay: the paper allows air to flow freely through, helping decay. As before, urine will assist the process.

---

applying it in these months is that it can be applied to established beds or borders before most of the herbaceous plants have started into growth. However, if an application is not possible at this time, then it is better to apply it at other times of the year than not at all – except obviously in the summer months when the soil is dry or even parched.

The mulch should be applied to the surface of the soil some 2 to 3in (5 to 8cm) deep; this gives the garden a well tended look, and to a certain extent prevents the emergence of weeds (*see* Figure 1).

To encourage almost total eradication of weeds prior to the application of the mulch, the beds and borders can be covered with whole newspapers, their edges overlapping by at least an inch on all sides: if you fail to do this the weeds will come up in the gaps between the papers creating a draught-board effect. Papers should be cut so they form neat collars round the base of trees, shrubs, roses and fruit bushes. Where the paper covers herbaceous plants, nicks should be cut to allow the emergence of shoots. This may sound labour-intensive, but it isn't really, and saves a lot of work in the late spring, summer and autumn; plus the plants do appreciate the cool root run it provides. Newspapers cannot be laid on top of the soil where bulbs are due to emerge, however.

After its application the paper starts to decay, which in turn allows the compost to permeate the soil. As it does so, it assists moisture retention and aeration at the same time. As you apply your mulch each year, you will find that over the years it takes longer to disappear, and there will come a time when you can reduce the amount that you apply possibly down to just an inch. But never miss a year's application, because a mulch is a good soil conditioner, and also because it gives the garden a well-tended appearance, and shows that the owner really cares for it.

There are several types of mulching material available, as described below.

Spent Mushroom Compost

This is the waste material from mushroom farms. It is not expensive to purchase either by the bag or lorry load, but obviously the latter is the cheaper. Its other main advantage is that it is very light in weight, enabling it to be wheeled to any part of the garden with ease. Once applied and wetted by natural or other means, it takes on a lovely earthy brown colour, making it attractive to look at and giving the garden a well cared-for feel, and it forms a natural background to the many greens of the plants emerging through it.

Mushroom compost does contain lime or chalk, but the quantity in it is very low, and it takes many years to alter the pH of the soil by 0.1 per cent.

Fig 2. A cross-section of a home-made compost bin. Material of different kinds is in layers to aid air circulation.

Garden Compost

Sadly garden compost varies enormously in quality. Ideally as it is removed from the compost heap it should resemble dark crumbly fruit cake and be warm to the touch. If it is not of this consistency, it may be that it has been removed too early from the container: it will therefore have failed to heat up sufficiently to destroy any weed seeds, and this could create a problem in the forthcoming growing season, when young weed seedlings will start to appear through or in the mulch.

Farmyard Manure

Like garden compost, farmyard manure must be stacked to decompose enough to generate sufficient heat to destroy weed seeds. If this has been done it is ideal mulch. If friends or neighbours have stables or farms they may be willing to give it to you free or for a minimal charge to cover the costs of loading and delivering it, unless you offer to do this yourself. It is applied at the same depth as the mushroom compost.

Bark

Bags of bark mulch can be purchased from garden centres or horticultural sundriesmen; if large quantities are required, it can be delivered loose by lorry. Like spent mushroom compost, it is weed-free and light to wheel around. If applied on an annual basis it can leach nitrogen from the soil, but this can be corrected by applying dressings of Gromore and fish, blood and bone to the surface of the soil before applying the mulch in the spring. Its cost is its only disadvantage, but for small gardens this may not be a determining factor, and garden centres often have special offers in the early spring such as buy three bags and get a fourth one free!

Spent Hops

If you have a local brewery near you it is worth contacting them to see if they sell spent hops once the beer-making process has been completed; and

Raised beds can be used successfully in vegetable gardening as well as ornamental gardening.

because they have lorries available, delivering should not be a problem. It is sterilized in the brewing process, is light to handle, and has the added advantage that for three or four days after applying it, it exudes a delicious beery aroma.

Other Alternatives

There are other options besides the above mulches, but they are usually localized. However, they are seriously worth considering if you can get your hands on them. Spent coffee grounds from coffee importers is one such option; and shoddy, which is the waste by-product from fabric manufacture, is marvellous for the retention of moisture – although a note of caution: unless it is wetted as soon as it is applied, it may be blown about in a strong wind, and it is beloved by birds as a nesting material. Also,

Above: Raised beds can be made from treated wood.

Fig 3. Cross-section of a raised bed.

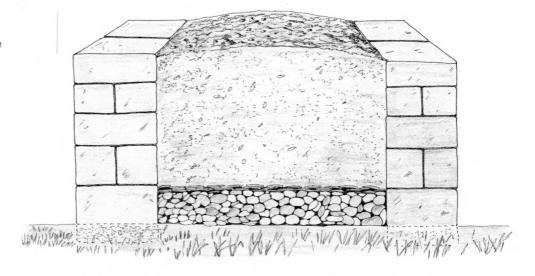

more and more local authorities are recycling waste garden material from residents' houses, composting it, and then offering it for sale.

You do not have to use the same compost year in, year out; in fact there is a great deal to be said for varying it, as this prevents a build-up of any undesirable elements, chemical or otherwise, in the soil.

RAISED BEDS

Sometimes the gardener has to deal with a site that is disturbed, whether this is by natural means – for example, regular localized flooding – or continual erosion, or overspill of yet more sticky clay from higher surrounding areas. In such cases it may be necessary to consider the construction of raised beds to allow cultivation in a more or less conventional manner. Where the site is all solid clay to start with, the construction of a few raised beds would be a quick way of getting the garden started.

On a long-term basis, if the bulk of the planting in the beds is of a permanent nature, raised beds can very quickly give the garden a very established appearance.

Raised Beds and Garden Design

Raised beds can, by their very nature, add greatly to the design of the garden. Each bed can be of a different height to its neighbours, the width can also vary, and they can be angular or curved, or both. They can have indentations in their sides to allow a seat to slot in without spoiling the overall design concept. If planting holes are left in the sides of the beds as they are constructed, this helps to soften the effect and negates the feeling of a box with planting only on its surface.

If a bed has only vegetables growing on its surface, and if these are only a temporary planting,

Rockrose (Helianthemum).

Raised vegetable beds separated with paths will allow the gardener easy access to tend to plants.

then permanent plants such as alpines or ferns can grow in the holes in its sides. If the beds are kept at the same height, then upright posts can be fixed into them and joined together by horizontal posts of the same thickness, and a pergola can be formed, which gives interest to the design and provides additional growing space – plants can grow up them and along them – which in turn provides shade to what is normally an exposed position, particularly if a space has been made in one of the beds to accommodate a seat. However, if the beds are of different heights, then the pergola design never seems right.

Where seats are inserted it is a good idea to plant plants that are fragrant near to them, so that the perfume can be enjoyed. However, when doing this,

ADVANTAGES OF RAISED BEDS

- They are a way of letting disabled gardeners garden.

- They are perfect to introduce children to gardening, as they are small enough overall to relate to a child's own small world.

- They are useful for containing a water feature in a garden where children are about, as being raised above ground level they cannot fall in. A water feature constructed near the house makes it even more enjoyable, as fish and other occupants can be viewed at any time of the year; as well as birds coming to drink or bathe, butterflies and dragonflies will be frequent summer and autumn visitors.

be very selective because plants such as *Daphne odora marginata* can become overpowering.

Constructing Raised Beds

As with any other part of the garden, raised beds need attention, so they must never be so wide that it is not possible to reach the centre from all sides, so that weeding and planting can be comfortably carried out. Their overall height should not exceed the waist height of the person who normally tends them, and preferably a little lower.

The beds can be made of wood that has been treated to withstand deterioration from continual moisture being present inside the container, or from stone, brick, breeze blocks painted a suitable colour, inverted turves (but this must only be thought of as a temporary measure, as they will col-

lapse in a few years), and peat blocks that will last for many years and look well when planted with acid-loving plants and ferns. Cover the base of the raised bed with a layer of rubble to help improve drainage (*see* Figure 3).

The composition of the growing medium within the beds depends upon what you intend to grow in them; for example, annuals such as vegetables and bedding plants, or perennials such as trees, shrubs and herbaceous plants. (Alpines, incidentally, would find it difficult to survive even on an improved clay soil.) Suitable growing mediums for all these plants can be found at your local garden centres. It is not necessary to fill the whole bed with the growing medium; as much as one third can be filled with drainage material, a second third with inverted turves, and the final third with the growing medium.

CHAPTER 2

Protection from the Wind

Having got your clay soil into a friable working condition, the last thing you want is to have it continually drying out due to the ravages of the wind, so a solution must be found to this problem. The answer is not to put up a solid boundary all round the property, because if you do this the wind will bounce against it, then rise over it, and still land with its full force on the planting below, with devastating effect.

You need to put up 'screens' that will allow the wind to filter through them, and these can be man-made or natural. Any man-made screen will inevitably be of solid materials, such as brick, stone, blocks or timber. If you drive through the Cotswolds, Yorkshire Dales, Devon or Cornwall, you rarely see boundary walls in excess of 3ft 6in (1.05m). These give protection from the wind, but their relatively low height allows the wind to blow over their tops into surrounding areas without causing damage to crops. They are also substantial enough that livestock can find a measure of shelter at their base.

CREATING SHELTER AND PRIVACY

To create boundaries at this height in gardens might help against the ravages of the wind, but would give no sense of privacy. We are still very much of the mindset that an 'Englishman's home is his castle' and must be protected against prying eyes, and this frequently means erecting boundaries of up to 6ft (nearly 2m) in height. As we have seen, solid boundaries of this height do nothing to com-

Flowering shrubs can give protection as well as being decorative.

promise the effects of a strong wind, so in their place are used protective screens such as wattle: these are made from strips of willow (*Salix*) or hazel (*Corylus*), woven horizontally through upright supports of the same material, long enough to be driven into the ground. As the strips are of varying thickness the wind can filter through the gaps, causing no harm to planting or people on the other side. Unfortunately, wattle screens have a short shelf life, and often start to disintegrate after five years; they are also expensive. Nevertheless, their great advantage is that a living screen can be planted on the garden side, and will have established itself by the time the hurdles do finally disintegrate. Certainly on a very exposed site this is the answer.

Fencing can be used, but again, do not erect a solid type; go instead for what is known as 'interwoven': in a way this is a version of hurdles, as there are always varying widths of slat, which leaves gaps between each row, allowing at least some of the wind to funnel through. Unfortunately, planting a living screen adjacent to it is not the answer, because it will be growing in virtual shade and when the panels are eventually removed, it will have very little greenery because it will have had so little light.

Where a more permanent barrier is erected, such as a brick, block or stone wall, it is advisable to keep its height as low as possible. Such barriers are expensive to erect, but they can become an important feature of the design, and may also provide a support on which climbing flowering plants can grow, or fruit trees can be supported.

Where such permanent structures are erected on clay soils, do ensure that the correct foundations are put in place, because of all the soils, clay is the one

Left: Trees and Carpinus Betulus *with foreground planting of* Phlomis Fruticosa.

Opposite: The shrub L. Ovalifolium Aureum *makes a good screening plant.*

most prone to subsidence problems. Furthermore, if you are going to erect the walls yourself it would be advisable to contact the building inspector at the local council offices who knows the area well and would give you advice on the type of foundations to use. At the time of writing, planning consent is not required for walls that do not exceed 6ft 6in (2m) in height.

LIVING SCREENS

The choice here is endless, but the following plants are the most suitable to grow on clay soils.

Hornbeam

Carpinus betulus (hornbeam) is one of the few plants that truly enjoys growing on clay soil. It rapidly establishes itself, and over a two- to three-year period after planting, starts to make a good thick screen. Its foliage is dark green and heavily veined; it turns to a pale yellow in the autumn and then to a silky grey, hanging on well into the late winter. Ideally it prefers a sunny, open position, but it will tolerate some shade. Plant during the dormant period between November and March, using bare root plants. Hornbeam can be spaced up to 3ft (90cm) apart, and closer if you need a more immediate effect.

Beech

Fagus sylvatica (beech) grows well in any soil that is not waterlogged; like the hornbeam, it prefers open situations to shady ones. It has oval leaves that are pale green when young, turning to dark green when mature. Its autumn colouring is a rich golden yellow turning to orange brown. The foliage stays on throughout the winter until pushed off by the new emerging buds in the spring. Planting distance is the same as for the hornbeam.

Common Thorn

Crataegus monogyna (common thorn) has broadly oval, deeply lobed, glossy dark green leaves. Fragrant white flowers are produced in the spring, and the foliage turns to lemon yellow before falling in the autumn. *Crataegus* prefers an open situation, but will grow in most places provided the ground is not waterlogged. Thorn is a superb hedge for growing in exposed places, or for growing by the sea. Ideally, thorn should be grown in a double staggered row with plants put in at 2ft (60cm) spacing, again using bare root plants.

As well as *monogyna* there are many other varieties that make excellent hedges; one that stands out is *C. crus galli*, the cockspur thorn. It will stand

the bleakest of situations, and will deter both humans and animals from trying to get through it because the thorns are numerous, long and curved. Its foliage is dark, glossy green, and turns to orange, to red and eventually to crimson before falling. It has fragrant white flowers in late spring, followed by bright red fruits that last well into the winter.

Privet

Like the *crataegus*, *ligustrum* (privet) consists of many species and varieties. Although strictly speaking they are all classified as deciduous, in mild winters they can hold on to their foliage, becoming semi-evergreen. *L. lucidum* and *L. japonicum* are two evergreen varieties, but are not really suitable for exposed or draughty positions. In the summer they all carry strangely scented white flowers, not enjoyed by most. There are variegated forms in both silver and gold.

Ligustrum thrives on well drained clay soil, and even on a very dryish one. It can require clipping more than once in a season, and as it carries black fruits in the winter months, this can sometimes be a problem. Plant 2ft (60cm) apart in the autumn, or

at other times if you buy pot-grown plants – although if you do this, keep them well watered until they are firmly established.

Sea Buckthorn

As with the thorn, *Hippophae rhamnoides* (sea buckthorn) is an excellent subject for both exposed and coastal positions. It has narrow silvery leaves, tiny yellow flowers in the spring, and if a combination of male and female plants is used, the flowers give rise to bright orange fruits in the autumn, which are a striking feature against the silvery leaves. Like *C. Crus galli*, it is extremely thorny, keeping intruders out. Normally purchased as pot-grown plants, they are planted at 3ft (90cm) spacing.

Purple-Leaved Plum

If you want to bring some background colour into the garden, then *Prunus spinosa 'purpurea'* (purple-leaved plum) is the one to select, as it has bright red foliage in the early spring, eventually turning to reddish purple. It has bright pink flowers in the spring followed by blue fruits in the autumn. This screen will give good, sturdy, quick growth even in the most exposed positions. Plant 2ft (60cm) apart, using either bare root plants or pot-grown ones.

EVERGREEN SUBJECTS
Yew

Taxus baccata (yew) is a fully hardy tree, with needle-like flattened dark green leaves. Once established, this screen offers a feeling of permanency to even the newest of gardens. Yew does well on clay soil in exposed positions. It is alleged to be slow growing, but if foliar fed (*see* page 11) it can put on 1 to 1.5ft (30 to 45cm) of growth in a season. This is a perfect foil for any type of planting put in front of it, but it is not advisable to use as a boundary hedge where neighbours have livestock, as yew can be poisonous to horses, sheep and cows. It is interesting that the foliage is now used in some cancer treatments. Plant 3ft (90cm) apart, using containerized plants only: do not be tempted to use bare root plants. Yew must be kept well watered until established, and it appreciates mulching, as this provides it with a cool root run.

Laurel

Prunus laurocerasus (common laurel) forms a good solid hedge even on the poorest of clay soils. It is fast growing and can put on at least 3ft (90cm) a year in height. Because it is so accommodating, its value as a living screen has often been underestimated. If it is allowed to grow up to 6ft (2m) in height the size of the leaf looks to be in the right proportion for the hedge. The leaves are green with a shiny surface.

Prunus must be cut with secateurs, and never mutilated with shears or hedge cutters; if the leaves are cut across, they turn yellow and die. You can buy bare root plants, which should be planted in either September or October while the soil is still warm, or in April and May as the soil is starting to warm up; however, it is preferable to plant container-grown plants. Plant 3ft (90cm) apart; a single row is quite sufficient to make a superb screen.

Holly

Ilex (holly) is, in many respects, the ideal hedging subject for gardening on clay. It grows in either sun or shade, but those varieties bearing variegated foliage do best in full sun or semi-shade. If you need a wind protector, use the common holly (*Ilex aquifolium*), with wavy, dark green leaves, glossy and sharply spined. It bears bright red berries in the early winter months on the female plants. Hollies are normally unisexual – they are male or female – so to get berry production it is necessary to plant both sexes. As with most evergreens, clipping is carried out by hand using secateurs.

Because a plant is listed as being evergreen, gardeners assume that the plant does not drop its leaves, but after the leaves have been on the plant for three or four years they fall to the ground to be replaced by new foliage so the plant never looks bare. Unless you are content to let the dead leaves lie at the base of the hedge, you have to collect them and this can be a painful job, so make sure you wear strong leather gloves.

Depending upon the size of plants you start with, the spacing will be from 1.5 to 3ft (45 to 90cm). As with the yew screen, holly can be foliar fed, so smaller plants can be used; this may be beneficial if there is a long length of living screen to plant.

To give added interest to the holly hedge, two varieties of the hardy cyclamen could be planted at its base: *C. hederifolium*, which flowers in the autumn, and *C. coum*, a spring-flowering variety. These will soon naturalize themselves.

CONIFERS

Conifers are another suitable hedging plant for growing on clay, and there are several varieties to choose from: true cypress (*Cupressus*), thuja, yew (*Taxus*) – already mentioned – and cypress (*Chamaecyparis*) are the best of these.

When *Cupressocyparis Leylandii* was first introduced to the market it was greeted with great acclaim. It has vigorous upright growth, putting on a minimum 3ft (90cm) of growth in a season. It has dark green foliage, which is spray-like in formation. But a word of warning: in two years it will have attained 6ft (2m) or more in height, and it will have become very dense – and the trouble doesn't stop there, as it just keeps on growing. So unless its sides and top are cut several times in the growing season, it becomes a nightmare, not only to you, but to your neighbours as well.

The other problem is that to put on this amount of growth, its roots have to search far and wide to find the necessary moisture and nourishment, thus depriving plants growing adjacent to it of the moisture and food they need to survive: so be very wary of planting *C. Leylandii*. You have been warned!

GARDEN SHRUBS

Some of our garden shrubs also make excellent screens, and the following are good choices for growing on clay.

Viburnum

Viburnum tinus (laurustinus) does well in any conditions of light or shade. It has dark green, oval-shaped leaves. From October through to March, the buds are a delightful shade of pink; they open to become clear white flowers, and the overall appearance is a cloud of flattish heads. These are followed by very small, blackish fruits later in the season. Clip after flowering. Plant 3ft (90cm) apart.

Viburnum farreri and its many varieties has very upright growth, so is perfect for a hedge. It is deciduous, with bronze foliage when young, which eventually turns to dark green. From autumn and through the winter it carries fragrant white or pink button-shaped flowers. Plant at 3ft (90cm) spacing, and prune to shape. If you find that eventually it starts to go bare at the base, prune some of the older stems back hard to encourage new growth.

Cotoneaster

Cotoneaster x 'Cornubia' and *C. x watereri* both make excellent informal screens. They are semi-evergreen, being very decorative in the autumn and winter as they carry clusters of bright red fruits. Hand clip to an informal shape in the spring. As they are vigorous growers, planting can be as far as 6ft (2m) apart in a single row. If planted in a series of linked 'Ss' across the rear boundary of a property, additional interest results, and trees can be planted in the recesses, thereby giving additional protection to the garden – so important when gardening on clay.

Mexican Orange Blossom

Choisya ternata (Mexican orange blossom) is much hardier than presupposed, and does well on clay provided it is given some additional drainage material at planting time. It is evergreen, with aromatic glossy green leaves, and bears very fragrant, white flowers that appear in late spring and again in the autumn. Clip when the spring flowering has finished, again with secateurs.

Forsythia

Forsythia intermedia x 'Beatrix Farrand' and *Forsythia x intermedia* 'Lynwood' are both varieties that have very erect growth. They make excellent living screens, carrying clouds of yellow flowers in early

This Chaenomeles *'Knaphill Scarlet' will not grown quickly, but once established will make an effective screening plant.*

spring, followed in the autumn by a display of pale lemon as the leaves turn from green before falling to the ground. As soon as flowering has finished they should be trimmed to shape. They can be planted as bare-rooted plants in October or November, or as container-grown plants at any other time. They should be planted 5ft (1.5m) apart.

Flowering Quince

Chaenomeles (flowering quince) is another subject for an exposed site. There are several varieties, including 'Crimson and Gold' and 'Knaphill Scarlet', and the colour range runs from white to pink to several shades of crimson and scarlet. Initially this is not a fast grower, but once it has established itself it grows well, and is certainly a good choice for growing on clay.

IN SUMMARY

So as the various options presented above suggest, there are ways of protecting your garden from the ravages of the wind, and while you choose one option for the boundary, another may present itself to be used as a screen or screens within the garden; in this way the garden may be presented as a series of rooms, which is a very popular concept in garden design at present.

CHAPTER 3

Planting

After getting the soil into a friable working condition in which plants will grow and thrive, the next important aspect of gardening on clay is the actual planting.

Correct planting is vital in a plant's life. To plant incorrectly is a disaster. Planting has to be carried out correctly and certainly not rushed, as some plants may remain *in situ* for hundreds of years – oak and beech trees for example.

The first step before any planting is undertaken is to ensure that the plant is going to be happy where you intend to plant it. Be sure to ask yourself if the soil is the right type for the plant you are considering. There is no point in putting an acid-loving plant on an alkaline soil or vice versa, a sun-loving plant in a shady position or vice versa, a moisture-loving plant in a hot dry position or vice versa, etc. So many people go to a garden centre, see a plant in flower, fall in love with it, buy it, take it home, plant it without looking at the planting instructions on the label and are surprised when it dies.

PLANTING METHODS

Having decided you have got the right plant for where you intend to put it, you need to excavate a sufficiently large hole to accommodate its roots comfortably both in depth and width. An example of bad planting is when bedding plants are put in with a trowel which has more or less taken out a scoop of soil to get the plant in and no more.

Conventional planting

Having excavated the hole there are two different

Careful planting will ensure that plants thrive.

It's easy to fall in love with a plant at the garden centre, but after planting make sure that it is tended properly until it is well established.

ways of carrying out the planting; the first is the conventional way, i.e. incorporate some well-forked compost into the bottom of the hole and, depending upon the size of the hole, up to two handfuls of

a general fertilizer, again well forked in. Place the plant in the centre of the hole and fill in the space between it and the walls of the hole with the soil that was excavated to make the hole firm with your foot and then water in. The main problem with this method is that quite often the compost and fertilizer has leached down through the soil before the plant roots have been able to reach it.

The sodden newspaper method

The second method has come about very much with possibility of climate change in mind and has proved to be very successful over the last few years. Prior to planting give the plant or plants a thorough soaking, excavate the planting hole as before then line the hole both bottom and sides with sodden wet newspapers. Select newspapers that are mainly black and white and do not have shiny surfaces. Each newspaper used should be at least twenty-four pages thick. Ensure that the papers lining the sides of the hole are at least one inch below the surface of the soil and very sodden.

Proper aftercare will ensure that plants thrive and continue to look stunning.

Do not put any compost or fertilizer at the bottom of the hole, but place the plant directly onto the sodden wet newspaper then, as with the conventional method, fill in with the previously excavated soil. Then apply a surface dressing of compost and fertilizer, which will gradually work its way down through the soil reaching the plant's roots when it is most needed. Do not water the plant in after planting as it was already wet when it was planted. This will give it time to allow its roots to begin searching for moisture, leading to healthy root production which in turn leads to a healthy plant able to combat pests and diseases.

The sodden newspaper takes up to eighteen months to decay and during this period as it dries out it attracts moisture from the soil surrounding it and under it, much as blotting paper or kitchen towel will do, thus ensuring the newly planted plant always has a supply of moisture available for its use.

If you are planting a small plant such as a lettuce or petunia the method is just the same but obviously the paper should be cut into six or eight squares but still keeping the same thickness as before. The plants should be watered thoroughly before planting and then not for two or three days afterwards.

Plants that are to be containerized, i.e. plants that are to be grown in a pot, tub, basket or other type of container, whether on a temporary or permanent basis, can be treated in exactly the same way using the newspaper method. Line the container, both base and sides, with sodden wet newspaper ensuring that the paper is at least one inch below the surface of the soil. If it isn't buried then the rays of the sun will strike it and dry the moisture out. By using the paper this not only provides a cool root run but also reduces the frequency of watering.

Similarly, if you are growing runner beans or sweet peas in a trench the lower third of the trench can be filled with sodden wet newspapers, they can be a mixture of all kinds, and again do not use shiny ones. This has two advantages; if the trench is excavated in the early winter, the newspapers put in and then the trench filled, the newspaper has a chance to decay through the winter. By the spring when the seeds or plants are ready to be put in, the decaying process will have started to warm the soil above it which in turn provides a welcoming environment for the start of rapid root growth. The sodden newspaper also provides a ready supply of moisture to the plant's roots as required.

There is a condition in the early summer known as 'July drop' when the night-time temperature drops considerably leading the flowers on the runner beans and sweet peas to drop off. It has been found that the decaying newspapers send up heat through the soil into the atmosphere to prevent this happening.

AFTERCARE

Having carried out the planting, do not, as so many people do, think that's it. Maybe it is for the non-permanent occupants of the garden, but the semi- or permanent occupants must receive continual tender loving care during their residency, i.e. they must be fed and mulched on a regular basis.

CHAPTER 4

Lawns

Lawns are an essential element of any traditional British garden, but they should thrive much better than their actual appearance in many a garden might suggest. Once laid or sown, lawns respond readily to continual tender loving care – which unfortunately they seldom receive. They need nurturing, and failure to do this on clay soil is very quickly made obvious by cracks of varying lengths and widths appearing at the first hint of drought conditions. And if a lawn doesn't grow vigorously, weeds, whether airborne or from adjacent beds and borders, soon take over. Moreover if drought conditions continue for any length of time, weeds will remain the only sign of vegetation – although the grass will start growing again with the first autumnal rains.

PREPARATION

Prior to the sowing of grass seed or the laying of turves, the lawn site must be thoroughly prepared: by doing this the effects of drought conditions might possibly be delayed for several weeks or longer. To this end the soil should be cultivated to at least a depth of 12in (33cm), and more if possible.

The texture of clay soil in the winter and right through to spring is mostly very heavy, and if the soil has only been cultivated to the depth of a spade blade or less, over the years a solid pan would form below this level. This would then make the passage of water, bacterial interaction and air flow through the soil virtually impossible. Once this pan has been fractured, however, plant growth is remarkable.

Often where the site has been built on previous-

A well-tended lawn is an essential element of the British garden.

ly, the contractor's dumper trucks and other vehicles will have gone backwards and forwards, and would have made the ground even worse for the cultivation of lawn. One has only to visit such a site in the winter when there are puddles everywhere, to see how difficult it is for the water to drain away.

Having cultivated the soil, apply Claybreaker, a pelleted soil conditioner, a blend of organic matter and gypsum. It makes the soil flocculate – that is, it causes it to break down from a heavy form to a crumbly texture, making it easier to work and helping to improve drainage, which enables bacteria and the worm population to flourish. It is not a fertilizer, but conditions the soil without affecting its pH (the acidity or alkalinity), and will improve even the heaviest clay, creating friable conditions and improving natural drainage, which in turn leads the soil to lose its coldness in the winter months, and to warm up earlier in the spring. This gives rise to earlier growth, leading to potentially earlier crops in the case of vegetables and fruit, and earlier flowers that we so desperately need after a dull, damp winter. This procedure also promotes the growth of grass.

Claybreaker can be used at any time of the year, but best results are obtained when it has been applied in the autumn to the area that has been rough dug or cultivated. The combined action of an application of Claybreaker and the effects of winter frosts will help to promote a good soil structure by the spring. Claybreaker is applied at 200g per square metre (6oz per square yard). Very heavy soils will benefit from a further application at the same rate in the following spring, prior to the sowing of grass seed or the laying of turf. Where there is an existing lawn that requires improvement, an application of Claybreaker should be given in late October or November, after the lawn has been

LAYING TURVES

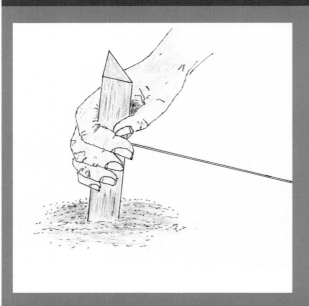

Use string stretched between pegs to mark out the area to be turfed over.

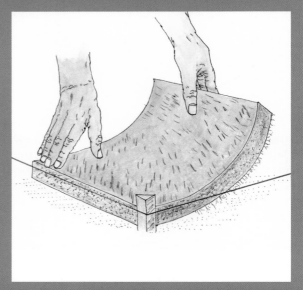

Lay out the turves along the edge of the boundary, then lay a second row, making sure they lie flat and are tight up against the edge of the first row.

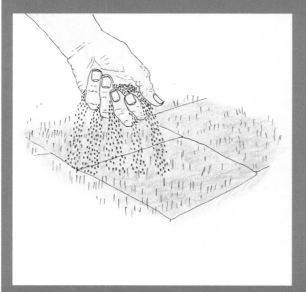

Once the turves are all in place, you can sprinkle a lawn top dressing over the surface.

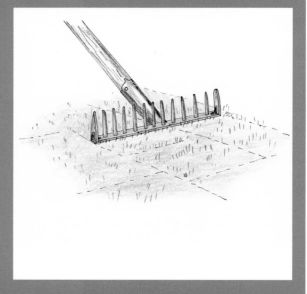

Use the back of a rake to work the top dressing into the joins and to ensure that the finished lawn lies flat.

Using a rake to remove moss and dead material.

scarified, followed by spiking or hollow tining, which will help to aerate the lawn.

CARING FOR ESTABLISHED LAWNS

Established lawns can be fed with Claybreaker. If a fertilizer is needed, chicken fertilizer pellets are readily obtainable from garden centres or horticultural sundriesmen. If these are sprinkled directly on to the lawn, three to four weeks prior to cutting it in the spring, at the rate of a handful per square metre (or yard), this will put it into good heart for the rest of the growing season. It is advisable to apply the pellets every year in the spring.

Having carried out the various suggestions discussed above, it then only needs for the lawn to be mown regularly, and the edges to be neatly clipped at the same time, and it will become the centrepiece of the garden, rather than something to apologize for!

FRAGRANT LAWNS

An alternative to the conventional lawn is a fragrant lawn, consisting of thyme (*Thymus serphyllum*),

AERATING THE LAWN

A very simple way of aerating a lawn is to mark it out in one metre (yard) wide strips, and then to stand on a garden fork at 1ft (30cm) intervals between each insertion, both widthways and lengthways. This will give a much deeper penetration than that given by some mechanical or hand-propelled machines.

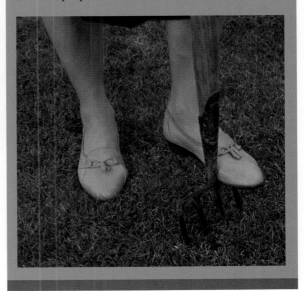

peppermint (*Mentha requienii*) and chamomile (*Anthemis nobile* 'Treneague'). Once this has become established, it is very easy to maintain as it requires no mowing, and because its growth is so dense and covers the ground, weed seeds find it virtually impossible to get a hold and become established. It stands up to drought conditions very well, and has the added merit that when it rains or is walked on it exudes the most delicious fragrance.

Prior to planting, soil preparation is just the same as for a conventional lawn. The thyme, peppermint and chamomile are purchased as 'plantlets', small plants grown in individual pots; these can be purchased from herb nurseries or garden centres during April and May. They are planted out 12in (33cm) apart, and can be a mixture of all three varieties, or only one if you prefer. They need to be kept well watered until established, and if this is done, within six weeks they will have joined up. One

Tender loving care will ensure that your lawn remains green and lush.

of the obvious advantages of this type of lawn is that it can be planted on a steep bank. Not only does it require minimal maintenance, but it roots so deeply into the soil that it prevents subsidence occurring, and once the ground is covered by its foliage, weed seeds find it very difficult, if not impossible, to find anywhere to flourish.

SEED LAWNS AND TURF LAWNS

When putting down a new, conventional lawn it is always a difficult choice to make as to whether it should be seed or turf.

Using Seed

Firstly, consider the merits of seed:

- It is less expensive than turf.
- In the long run it probably gives the better lawn.

- Because of the numerous varieties of grass seed available, you can choose the right one for your garden, taking into account features such as sun or shade, dry or damp, from varieties that you know will do well on the soil *in situ*.

It can take anywhere from twenty-one to forty-eight days for the seeds to germinate, depending on what time of the year they are sown. Moreover, after germination has taken place, a further six to eight weeks must elapse before it can be used. So patience must prevail.

Choose a hard-wearing seed that will be able to cope with children's activities and dogs or other animals. The seed must also be treated against bird predation, because otherwise much of it will be eaten before germination takes place; this will result in bare patches occurring that require reseeding, making it even longer before the lawn can be used. During the germination period and subsequent establishment, the lawn must be kept well watered at all times: it must never be allowed to dry out.

You might like to consider a grass seed seldom used in this country: New Zealand fescue. This grass has an unusual habit in that, unlike conventional grasses that grow upwards, this grass grows horizontally, thus requiring the minimum of mowing if you are a tidy gardener, or none if you are not. Maybe that is why it is not written about so much in the gardening press or on television, as the mowing machine manufacturers would not be thrilled by its publicity. For similar reasons, the seed is rarely available in garden centres. However, it can be obtained from agricultural suppliers.

New Zealand fescue is more expensive than conventional seed, but it is applied at 1.5oz per square yard against the normal application of 2oz. It is also very drought-tolerant, still retaining its greenness albeit with a reddish tinge to it, though this is not unpleasant to look at, and quickly vanishes at the first rainfall.

Scientists have long sought to find a grass seed that is impervious to drought conditions, where the grass stays green whatever the growing conditions. At the beginning of the twenty-first century a breakthrough occurred when a DNA mutation was found in the grass species Festuca. 'Staygreen', as it has subsequently been named, has already been incorporated into amenity grass seed mixtures, and will soon be available to the general public.

Using Turf

Turf provides an immediate effect, but not sufficient to allow it to be used immediately by children or animals, as it needs time to root into the ground on which it has been laid, and also for the joins to marry up with each other.

Like everything else in life, you get what you pay for: thus the cheaper turves contain grasses such as rye grass that are coarse in texture and not easily cut with a mower – the blades of grass tend to bend over as the mower passes over them, bending back upwards when the mower has moved on. If the lawn is to serve a decorative rather than a functional purpose, a combination of fine grasses in the turf is what is required. Cumberland turf is a good example.

When turf is laid, it must be laid in a bonded pattern, as in bricklaying – the joins do not lie parallel, but are staggered. If it is not possible to lay all the turves in one day, those remaining should be covered with damp cloths or sacks to prevent them drying out; if this is not done, they will get curly edges, which makes it very difficult to bond with those already laid. Once the turf has been laid, like the seed, it must be kept well watered until it is established.

Do remember that whatever method you decide on to create your perfect lawn, at the end of the day the solution remains in your hands. It is not only the initial preparation, but the continual tender loving care that you give it in succeeding years that will make it successful.

CHAPTER 5

Trees

The majority of trees seen in this country will grow on clay soils, but they are not always suitable for medium- to small-sized gardens. Certainly *Aesculus* (horse chestnut) and *Quercus* (oak) would be overwhelming and cast too much shade. *Salix* (willow), *Populus* (poplar) and *Fraxinus* (ash) present a different kind of problem, as all three have very invasive root systems, and should never be planted less than 30ft (10m) from property, drains, driveways and paths. The root systems consume vast amounts of moisture, which in turn leads to subsidence, particularly on clay soils.

CHOOSING TREES FOR THE CLAY GARDEN

Sometimes it is a good idea to concentrate on one group of trees that you know do particularly well on clay soils. *Malus* (crab apples), *Prunus* (ornamental cherries) and *Sorbus* (mountain ash) are three good groups for growing on clay. All of these have the advantage of being beautiful when in flower, have superb autumn colour, and carry fruits or berries; some even have ornamental bark that comes into its own during the winter months.

Crab Apple

Let us first consider the crab apple (*Malus*). The best members of this family for garden display are as follows:

Malus Floribunda is a spreading tree with a dense

Opposite: Acer platanoides 'Crimson King'.
Right: Malus Floribunda *(otherwise known as the crab apple) bears striking pink flowers.*

head; at flowering time it is covered with pale pink flowers that open from tight red buds. The fruits are tiny, pea-shaped yellow crab apples. It has lovely autumnal tints.

Malus 'Golden Hornet' has a spreading habit, with dark green foliage that sets off the cup-shaped white flowers in late spring. In the autumn the branches are weighed down with a profusion of yellow crab apples that can be used to make excellent jam or jelly, or can simply be left on the tree for decoration.

Malus 'John Downie' is probably the best of all the crab apples as regards fruiting. The apples are red flushed cream, and are edible straight from the tree. Unlike the two previous varieties, it has a narrow conical shape. The spring foliage is bright green, which sets off the large white flowers superbly.

Malus 'Royalty' is a spreading tree with glossy purple foliage. Its flowers are crimson-purple, giving rise to dark red fruits in the autumn.

Ornamental Cherry

The ornamental cherries (*Prunus*) are a large family, and are ideal for providing interest over a long period. The following four varieties are excellent for growing on clay:

Prunus 'Amanogawa', commonly known as the poplar cherry due to its narrow, upright habit, has fragrant semi-double flowers in the spring, followed by beautiful autumnal tints. The leaves start yellow, then change to orange, finally turning red before they fall. Because of its narrow habit, it is perfect to be planted in a corner where it does not intrude into your neighbour's garden.

Prunus 'Pissardii' is a rounded, shaped tree. Its oval red leaves turn deeper red as the season progresses, becoming purple in the autumn. Pale pink flowers burst through the foliage in the early spring.

Prunus 'Spire' has an unusual vase-shaped habit. It

Above: Prunus *'Amanogawa' is also known as the poplar cherry.*

Right: Prunus *'Ukon' – one of the many varieties that will make a striking display in the spring.*

carries a profusion of soft pink flowers in the spring. The foliage is dark green at the start of the growing season, turning to the most wonderful orange-red at leaf fall.

Prunus 'Kursar' is a large spreading tree with deep pink flowers in early spring. Its summer green foliage turns the most brilliant orange before falling to the ground.

Mountain Ash

The Mountain Ash (*Sorbus*) family are grown for their foliage, flowers, attractive autumnal berries and colour. Note that those that bear leaflets as opposed to leaves do not do well on clay. The genus can furthermore be susceptible to the disease fireblight.

Sorbus aria 'Lutescens' starts off as an upright tree, but as the years go by it turns into a very impressive spreading tree. The young foliage is silvery, turning later to grey-green as it ages. White flowers in the spring are followed in the autumn by orange-red fruits, and the foliage turns lemon yellow before falling.

Sorbus sargentiana is a tree with white flowers in the spring and rounded red fruits in the autumn, when at the same time the mid-green leaves turn a brilliant red.

Sorbus hupehensis has blue-green leaflets that turn orange-red quite late in the season. Unusually it has white berries tinged with pink. This *Sorbus* is one of the few with leaflets that do well on clay.

Sorbus insignis also has leaflets – as many as twenty-three of them – oblong in shape and dark green in colour. It has large clusters of white flowers, giving rise to pink fruits that turn white as winter progresses.

OTHER TREES FOR THE CLAY GARDEN

Among others that could be considered for group plantings are the *Acers* (the maples), the *Crataegus* (the thorns or May trees) and the *Betulas* (the birches).

Single specimen trees could be selected from any of the groups above, or from the following list:

● *Amelanchier canadensis*

● *Cercis siliquastrum* (the Judas tree)

● *Gleditschia*, particularly the variety *triacanthos* (the honey locust tree); it has fern-like, glossy dark green leaves that turn yellow in the autumn.

● The *Robinia* family, especially the variety 'Frisia', because it has lovely golden foliage for the whole of the growing season.

With climate change in mind, two trees that would give our gardens a Mediterranean feel and do well on clay are *Paulownia*, with wonderful blue fox-glove-like flowers in early summer; and *Catalpa* that flowers in July and August with horse chestnut-like flowers. Both of these trees have large leaves, some 10in (25cm) in length and at least 6in (15cm) wide, so the foliage is a feature in itself the whole summer through. There is a variety of *Catalpa*

STAKING TREES

When young trees are first planted they need to be given support by staking.

Use a low stake to allow the tree some movement. The stake should be around 24in (60cm) high. Padded or buckle-and-spacer ties will prevent chafing to the young tree trunk.

called 'Aurea' which, as its name implies, has beautiful golden foliage all summer. Both the *Paulownia* and the *Catalpa* should be grown in isolation where their beauty can be admired. They make excellent specimen trees on lawns.

CARING FOR TREES

As trees are long-term occupants of the garden, they must be planted with care (*see* Chapter 3) and then should not be forgotten about, but fed annually. During their first two or three years after planting they must never be allowed to dry out, because if this happens there is no guarantee that they will survive, so keep a watch on them and water them before signs of stress appear.

Trees will become even more important as climate change becomes a reality, because as temperatures rise, the need for shade will become an essential requirement of our gardens, both by natural means and by man-made items such as umbrellas and awnings. So instead of planting a single tree we may be wiser to plant two, three or more. The sooner they are planted and become established the better, as not only will they provide us with much-needed shade, but they will also offer shelter for the plants growing under them.

CHAPTER 6

Shrubs

In the last few years interest in planting shrubs has grown enormously, as they are readily available, being container grown, and therefore can be planted at any time of the year. To see the shrub in flower, or displaying its autumn colour and covered in fruits or berries at the nursery or garden centre, is an incentive to purchase it, take it home and plant it.

However, while this may be the perfect solution to filling a gap or gaps in an existing border, it is not the perfect solution where new beds and borders are being made. To take home every week one or two shrubs as they appeal to you, means that you end up with a collection of plants that do not necessarily harmonize with each other. This might be because the colours of their flowers clash, if they flower at the same time, or their autumnal tints do not stand out as they should do in a well planned border. It is far better to draw up a scheme before you go out buying plants, and then stick to it!

The list of shrubs that will do well on clay soil is endless – in fact the topic of shrubs on clay merits a book to itself! However, to list them all is not the purpose of this book, and instead, twenty shrubs to grow on clay have been selected for their all-round value. As with trees, it is the initial preparation that you make at planting time, and their subsequent aftercare, that will enable the shrubs to give of their best. The correct pruning procedure for each shrub selected is given at the end of its description, and it is imperative that this is carried out so the shrub can be full of flower the following season.

Acuba Japonica crotonifolia.

VIBURNUMS

Viburnums are a large family consisting of both deciduous and evergreen varieties, and with careful selection you can have one of them providing interest in the borders every month of the year. Thus three varieties instead of one are suggested, as each deserves a place in the garden.

The first is *V. tinus* (laurustinus), an evergreen shrub, good for sun or shade. Its white flowers are followed by clusters of tiny, shiny black berries. The viburnum should be pruned to the required shape when flowering has finished, though this may mean that some of the berries may be lost. Should it be allowed to get out of hand, it can be cut back hard in April/May, after which it will quickly regenerate itself.

Viburnum 'Plicatum' (the Japanese snowball tree) is a dense, spreading shrub that is fully hardy. Its foliage is dark green, turning deep red-purple in the autumn. Dense, rounded heads of large, snow-white flowers – hence its common name – are borne along its branches in early summer. After flowering, remove as many of the branches that have flowered without spoiling its outline shape.

V. fragrans, syn *V. farreri* is deciduous, with a very upright habit and fully hardy. The oval-toothed leaves are pale green when they first emerge, turning to dark green. It produces clusters of white flowers in the autumn, and then at varying intervals through the winter and spring. It can get rather tall in a small garden, so when flowering has finished its top can be reduced by 2 to 3ft (60 to 90cm). It also gets very dense in its middle, so some of these stems can be removed almost to ground level after flowering.

BUDDLEIAS

Buddleia is a very large group of shrubs; they can be deciduous, semi-evergreen or evergreen, and they flower over a long period, depending upon the variety chosen. With climate change becoming even more of a possibility, the flowering period will be extended even further. Bearing this in mind, as with the viburnums, three varieties have been selected.

With buddleias, pruning is not the norm, because with such a long flowering period, to prune in the spring would preclude the flowering of *B. alternifolia* and *B. globosa* in May or June. So you must go by the golden rule of all pruning: if a plant flowers between 1 January and 30 June, prune after flowering; and if it flowers between 1 July and 31 December, prune in March or April.

B. alternifolia is a deciduous arching shrub with narrow, grey-green leaves and fragrant, lilac-pink flowers that appear in early summer. Once flowering has finished, prune away the shoots that have flowered, and any other stems that need to be shortened to produce the shape you require.

B. globosa is a very unusual flowering shrub in that it produces orange-coloured balls in early summer. It can be deciduous, or in mild winters can be semi-evergreen. Like the previous buddleia, it is pruned after flowering, cutting hard back the stems that have flowered.

This shrub looks very much at home in the wilder parts of the garden; it also looks superb when emerging from a group of silver-leaved shrubs such as *Hippophae rhamnoides* (sea buckthorn), which in the autumn also have orange-coloured berries, thus repeating the orange theme twice in one season. This theme can be further emphasized by planting two *Jackmanii* clematis at the base of the buddleia so they grow up and through it. In early autumn these produce purple flowers, which complement the orange berries of the *Hippophae*. The clematis should be pruned back each spring in March or April.

B. davidii is what most gardeners think of as being the conventional buddleia. There are many varieties that come in a wide colour range from white, primrose, and many shades of blue into pink and red. It is a very vigorous shrub, and if not pruned annually it can get out of hand. The pruning

should be carried out in March. It is fully hardy, like most buddleias, and has an arching habit. The leaves are long, lance-shaped, and dark green in colour, with a white felted underside. This group carries dense clusters of fragrant flowers in great profusion, and these are beloved by both bees and butterflies – hence its common name 'the butterfly bush'.

OTHER SUITABLE SHRUBS
Choisya ternata

Also known as Mexican orange blossom, this is an evergreen rounded shrub with aromatic, deep green leaves that are composed of three leaflets. Clusters of white flowers emerge in great profusion in the spring, and a second flowering, not so profuse, comes in the autumn. There are golden foliage

Right: Choisya temata *'Sundance'*.

Opposite: Buddleia alternifolia *has fragrant lilac-pink flowers.*

varieties, but these can be burnt by the sun if the summer is hot, and then look unsightly. Prune to shape with secateurs after flowering.

Photinia 'Red Robin'

A few years ago this shrub was rarely seen in our gardens, but it is rapidly becoming a firm favourite. It has evergreen, bold oblong leaves, and the new young red growths produced in the spring hold their colour for a long time. It has broad heads of five-petalled white flowers that appear soon after the emergence of red shoots, making an exciting contrast. It is spectacular when planted in groups of three or five, and used as an ornamental hedge. Prune with secateurs as required after flowering has finished.

Elaeagnus pungens 'Maculata'

This is an old variety that has stood the test of time. It is another evergreen, so important in formation planting, slightly spiny, and its glossy, dark green leaves have a deep yellow central patch. Fragrant, urn-shaped, creamy white flowers appear in mid to late autumn. Prune it to maintain shape as and when required. Sometimes shoots that are completely green appear, and these should be removed as soon as they are spotted.

Cotoneasters

These shrubs belong to a very large family, ranging from those that cover the ground, to almost tree-like specimens. Both deciduous and evergreen are included in this family. *C. Cornubia* is one of the most outstanding. It is semi-evergreen, in that in cold winters it can lose its leaves. It has an arching habit. Clusters of white flowers appear amongst its dark green leaves in the summer, followed by a wonderful display of bright red fruits that last well into the winter, as long as the blackbirds don't eat

them! Prune it in the dormant period to keep it in bounds, as it is very vigorous.

Abelias

This is a small family, but an extremely useful one, as abelias bring new interest into the border from midsummer to autumn. These are semi-evergreen shrubs with an arching habit, suitable for the middle or front of the border. They have branches carrying a profusion of lilac-pink flowers from July onwards. The best variety is Grandiflora. Prune if necessary in the spring to clear out the growth if it is getting too crowded, but an annual pruning is not necessary, and pruning is possibly only needed every second or third spring.

Mahonias

All mahonias are evergreen, and vary in height from 12in to 9ft (30cm to 3m). Their foliage is very architectural, having anything from twelve to twenty holly-like, spiny leaflets on each individual leaf. The flowers produced in late winter to early spring are very pronounced, upright racemes of fragrant yellow flowers. *M. bealei* is the most reliable of the group. Prune after flowering, removing the faded flowers and as much as possible of the stem beneath it to keep it in a good shape.

Exochordas

This group of deciduous shrubs is not commonly seen in gardens, but when they are, the immediate reaction is to want one for your own garden. They have very showy, white flowers in abundance in the spring, and they do best in full sun. After flowering, thin out the old shoots that have carried flowers. The best variety to grow is *Exochorda x macrantha* 'The Bride', as not only is it a free flowerer, but it has good autumn colour. It is commonly known as the bracelet tree.

Forsythia

Forsythia is an outstanding group of shrubs, their brilliant display of varying shades of yellow flowers announcing that spring has finally arrived. The flowers come out before the leaves. These shrubs are fully hardy, and prefer to grow out in the open in full sun. Their foliage is uninteresting, verging on the point of being dull, and were it not for their magnificent spring display of flowers, they would not be seen so frequently in gardens. The answer is to plant a climber to scramble through the branches to cover the leaves. After flowering, remove any stem that has just finished flowering, or at least shorten it back by half.

Potentillas

These deserve a place in every garden, whether big or small. They rarely exceed 3ft (90cm) in height, and are deciduous, usually forming a rounded bush, except for those with an erect habit: these are used to make dwarf hedges. The colour range is extensive, ranging from white, cream, yellow, apricot, tangerine and red.

    The reason they should be in every clay garden is that they start to flower in April and carry on right through into October and November. They enjoy being grown in an open sunny position, but the orange, red and pink cultivars prefer to be shielded from the midday sun. They are fully hardy, and should be pruned to retain their natural shape in the spring.

    P. 'Farrers White' is one of the best varieties, which generally bears flowers every day of the

season. As its name implies, the flowers are white, with lovely divided grey-green leaves.

Escallonias

The Escallonia family encompasses evergreen, semi-evergreen or deciduous trees or shrubs; however, in the average garden it is the evergreen shrubs that take pride of place. As with the Ceanothus, it is the varieties with the smallest leaves that are the hardiest. They are often grown as ornamental flowering hedges, particularly in coastal gardens where they provide both wind and sea spray protection. They prefer growing in full sun and are vigorous growers, benefiting from an annual feeding. They should be trimmed back when flowering has finished, and they lend themselves to topiary training. The flowers are produced in great profusion in late spring and early summer, and vary in colour from white and pink, to many shades of red. *E.* 'Apple Blossom', with its delicate-coloured flowers of pink and white, must come very high on the list.

Philadelphus

Philadelphus is deciduous, and when in leaf is not the most attractive of shrubs; however, when in flower it is gorgeous, for the quantity of flowers it produces, their pure whiteness and their superb fragrance. The other quality of Philadelphus is that it fills a gap between the end of the spring flowers

Opposite: Elaeagnus pungens maculata.

Left: Potentilla '*Tangerine*'.

as well as its free flowering habit, it decorates the garden with its shiny black berries in the winter. However, the star of the family of hypericums has to be the variety called 'Hidcote', a dense, bushy shrub with narrow, dark-green leaves; it is normally evergreen throughout the year. Its flowers are produced in great abundance from midsummer into autumn, and are large and golden yellow. When flowering has finished, the hypericum should be pruned back hard, reducing it to 6 or 9in (15 to 23cm) above ground level. Don't be frightened to do this: you will be astonished at how speedily new growth appears.

Cornus

Like the hypericums, cornus – or to give it its common name, 'dogwood' – come in all shapes and sizes, ranging from the low-growing *C. Canadensis*, to those that are either very large bushes or small trees. Many of them produce glorious coloured stems that are a highlight of any scheme planted for winter display. *C. alba* 'Elegantissima' is a classic example of this. It is a deciduous shrub, very vigorous, having bright red stems in the winter. Its foliage is grey-green, edged with white. The flowers, which are cream, are followed by small white fruits in the winter. This is a good shrub for growing not only in full sun, but also in semi-shade where it lightens up the bed or border. By the end of March the stems have lost their brightness, and this is the time to prune the previous year's growth hard back.

Syringa

The lilacs, when in flower, are beloved of cottage gardeners and are indeed a glorious sight, their smell pervading the air – though when not in flower they are dull green bushes. They can be enhanced by planting roses, clematis or honeysuckle to scramble through them. Lilac needs to be planted in an open, sunny position. Be sure to purchase plants that have been grown on their own roots, as

and the appearance of the summer blooms. There are several dwarf varieties, but it is the tall spire-shaped ones that give the best display, and of these, *P.* 'Virginal' is the best. After flowering has finished, cut back some of the older stems that have flowered to young growths, as these will develop and flower the following year.

Spiraea

This is a large group of shrubs, ranging from dwarf to very large, and flowering from March to October; at least one of the varieties will be in flower during this time. The flowers vary in colour from white and cream to pink and reds; possibly the best and certainly the most popular is the variety *Spiraea arguta* 'The Bride', one of the first spiraeas to flower in early spring. It has arching sprays of white flowers that look wonderful tumbling into any spring bulbs that are blue in colour. Pruning is very simple: just shorten those stems that have finished flowering to a new shoot below the faded flowers, and maintain a well trimmed shape.

Hypericums

This is an interesting group of shrubs, ranging from alpines that hug the ground, to medium-sized shrubs. Although most are sun lovers, one or two do well in semi-shade, or in the case of *H. x inodorum* 'Elstead', in shade. This is good, for grafted plants tend to become a nuisance with their ever-invading suckers.

Once flowering has finished, it is very important to remove faded flower heads because not only are they unsightly, but they also take strength from the plant as it tries to produce unwanted seed. To maintain the shape, prune once flowering has finished by shortening back growths and removing weak stems. Lilacs can become straggly, or they can grow beyond their allotted space, and this can be remedied by cutting them hard back in the winter months – often 6 to 8ft (2 to 2.4m) of main stems can be removed. *S.* 'Charles Joly' is one of the best, as it carries dense panicles of large, double, fragrant, deep purple-red flowers.

Deutzias

Deutzias come into flower at about the same time as philadelphus. Their colours are mainly pinks or whites, and they produce five-petalled flowers in great profusion, sometimes so profuse that at flowering time it is only the flowers that are visible – though they need to be grown in full sun to produce this abundance of flower. When flowering has finished, cut all flowering stems hard back. *D. x magnifica* can attain 8ft (2.4m) in height and become 6ft (2m) in width in a very short space of time. The flowers are pure white.

Hydrangea

Hydrangeas have been included here, again because of their diversity in flower shape and foliage. There is no reason why hydrangeas should not do well on clay soils, but as the first part of their name, Hydra – loving and needing water – implies, it is essential that at planting time plenty of moisture-retentive material is applied to the planting position, and in subsequent years each spring, that more is applied as a surface mulch. The flowers vary from being mop-heads, flat or cone-shaped, and go through the whole range of whites, creams, pinks and reds.

With such a diversity it is difficult to select one, but *H.* 'Annabell' must rate very highly, its creamy-white flowers becoming overlaid with lime green as they age. Remove faded flowers in the spring;

do not remove them in the winter, as they protect the emerging buds underneath. Removal of any dead wood and weak stems is all that is required. Do this at the same time as you apply the new season's mulch.

Euonymus

Euonymus (common name 'spindle tree') can be both deciduous and evergreen, dwarf, medium-sized and some as tall as small trees. *E. fortunei* 'Emerald and Gold' and *E. fortunei* 'Gaiety' are often seen in gardens as front-of-the-border shrubs, or used to make small formal hedges edging footpaths. Many of the deciduous varieties are renowned for their display of autumn colour and vivid fruits and berries. Indeed, *E. alatus* has been with us since Roman times, and appears in our natural hedgerows as a blaze of fire each autumn. *E.* 'Red Cascade', as its name implies, is a tall, pendant shrub with unbelievable autumnal colours and bunches of red and orange wax-like fruits.

CHOOSING YOUR SHRUBS

If the above twenty shrubs are planted they will give interest to beds and borders throughout the year. It is advisable not just to plant twenty single specimens, but from the list above include one or two groups of two or three planted together. By selecting from nurserymen's catalogues, or visiting gardens that are open under the National Gardens

Opposite: Mop-headed hydrangeas.

Above: Philadelphus *'Belle Etoile' has a striking display of fragrant flowers.*

Above: Syringa meyeri palibiniana.

Sambucus *'plumosa Aurea' will grow well on clay soil.*

CHAPTER 7

Herbaceous Plants

There is an enormous selection of perennials that are very happy growing on clay, so as in the previous chapter on shrubs, twenty of the best have been chosen. There is not the same winter impact as with shrubs, because most perennials are cut down to ground level at the end of the growing season – although if you are a bird lover, you might like to delay cutting them down until the spring, as many of the stems will support seedpods that supply valuable winter food for the birds. Photographers, too, might like to retain them, so they can take pictures of them covered in hoar frost.

No matter how small the garden is, perennials should never be planted singly, but in groups of three or five at least. Some of the vigorous ones, such as campanulas, asters (Michaelmas daisies), astrantia and the hardy herbaceous geranium, may need to be divided on a fairly regular basis, as otherwise they become overcrowded and their vigour is reduced, which in turn leads to the production of fewer flowers.

It is very important that in the spring, perennials are given a balanced fertilizer feed followed by a surface mulch. Next to this, deadheading – the removal of flowers as they start to fade – is almost as important, because if you do not let the flowers form seed, but remove them, the plant will send up new flowering stems to repeat the process all over again. Some, such as Nepeta (catmint), Alchemilla (lady's mantle) and Campanula (chimney bell flower), can be cut down three or four times in a season, thus giving a continuous display right into late autumn.

Oriental poppies are a classic example where cutting back after flowering is essential. In April,

Bergenia Cordifolia.

Papaver Orientale *need to be cut back after flowering.*

broad, lanced, toothed-shaped leaves appear, and shortly afterwards great big furry buds, which unfold to reveal dramatic tissue-paper-like flowers, often in the most amazing vibrant colours, usually with a black spot at the base of each petal. Sadly these only last for a very short period, and then the plant becomes dreary and uninteresting, eventually leaving a large gap in any planting scheme. Often as you walk round gardens in the summer you can see evidence of this. Some gardeners try to hide this gap by planting a dahlia or similar summer bedding plant, but this is not really the solution, and once flowering has finished it is far better to cut the poppy right back to ground level, including the foliage. Within two to three weeks new foliage will appear, followed by flowers, and if this is repeated two or three more times through the growing season, not only will you have a continual flower display, but the 'gap' is no longer a problem.

Mixed herbaceous planting.

Planting is ideally carried out in the early spring; before this, the planting position should have both a general fertilizer and a generous quantity of moisture-retaining compost incorporated into it. When planting has been carried out, surface mulch should be applied. Cutting back the dying flower stems and the foliage several times in a growing season causes the plant to use a great deal of energy in regeneration, so a foliar feed could also be given.

Not all perennials can be cut down, as they will only flower once in a season; *Iris germanica* and peonies are two plants that would hate such treatment. It is still advisable, however, to remove their fading flowers, unless their seedpods are of some decorative merit: leaving them on to form seed that you don't want will drain the plant of energy unnecessarily.

PESTS AND DISEASES

Perennials keep relatively free of pests and diseases, though some may have their own problems. For example, some varieties of aster may suffer from mildew, while most don't, so it is advisable to select the ones that are mildew-free. Slugs and snails are the main enemies of perennials, and unless you are an organic gardener this can usually be solved by sprinkling pellets round the plants. The manufacturers of these pellets have become so sophisticated that they can now provide ones that are not spoilt by showers of rain or consumed by birds. The important thing is to put the pellets down before the first signs of damage are spotted, not after it has happened!

For organic gardeners, one alternative is to put a surface of either crushed egg shells or coarse grit round the plants, as slugs and snails hate crawling over this. Another is to lay down string that has

Left: Campanula Persifolia.

Below: Lupins are a traditional favourite in the herbaceous border.

been smeared with Vaseline or mango butter in a circle round the plant or plants, as this is too slippery for them to glide over. Ensure that the circle is wide enough to accommodate all the plants' foliage within the circle. Yet another is to take the hulls of citrus fruits, once the flesh has been eaten, and fill them with a weak solution of beer: then bury them in the ground up to their surface, and slugs and snails, which can't resist beer, will climb down into them and drown, and can be disposed of the following morning. However, this method is not for the squeamish, because as many as twenty or thirty bodies can be found in each half of the fruit!

STAKING

Perennials that grow more than 2ft (60cm) in height will require staking, particularly in exposed gardens. Peonies in particular need support, even though they have strong, sturdy stems, because when their flowers open they are extremely heavy. The ideal method of staking is as follows: as soon as growth starts in the early spring, erect around the plant mound-like structures of twigs that have been pruned away from dormant trees or shrubs the previous winter – *Corylus* (hazel), *Tilia* (lime) and *Salix* (willow) are excellent for this purpose, as they

Hemerocallis *or the day lily is a herbaceous perennial.*

are very pliable. The base of the twig stems should be inserted firmly into the ground all round the plant or plants to be staked, and then tied together at their tops. Always ensure that the tops of the twigs are well below the height of the first flowers. If this operation is carried out really well, and it does take time and patience, the effort is undoubtedly worth it.

Not all perennials can be supported in this way, however, and delphiniums and dahlias, for example, may require each stem to be individually staked. The supports could be of strong bamboo canes; however, there are metal or plastic rings of various widths and height now available, with supporting legs so they can be inserted over the plant/plants to be staked. Like everything else in life, you pay your money and take your choice – so some of the cheaper ones rarely last more than two to three seasons, whereas some of the metal ones go on for ever. Obviously it is an expensive operation

to do the whole border all in one go, but perhaps they could become ongoing Christmas and birthday presents, something that you really need and will appreciate. Sometimes auction sales and reclamation yards are a good source of the metal ones – and you may even get a bargain!

CONTAINER PLANTS

Perennials make excellent outdoor pot plants, and can often stay in the same container for several years, as long as they are given an annual spring feed. *Hosta sielboldiana* makes a wonderful statement if dotted around the garden singly or in groups; it is also magnificent if arranged on each side of each tier of a flight of steps in a north-facing situation.

A planter containing a central planting of *Hemerocallis* (day lily) and an edging of *Stachys lanata* (lamb's tongue) becomes a focal point, as does a combination of *Iris germanica* (bearded intermediate) and *Hemerocallis*. *Agapanthus* is also an excellent long-lived container plant.

One final tip: when you start to divide your perennials because they have outgrown their allotted space, pot up some pieces, and then if you have any gaps in your beds or borders you can use them as 'gap fillers'.

THE BEST PERENNIALS TO GROW ON CLAY

Using some, or all, of the following selected plants should provide you with a very floriferous border, and of course you could add more of your own personal favourites to them. I have not included delphiniums, lupins, Sweet Williams and Canterbury bells in my selection of the best perennials, as quite often they tend not to last many seasons when grown on clay.

Acanthus

The common name for acanthus is 'bear's breeches'. It is a small family of semi-evergreen plants, with leaves that are large, deeply cut and shiny, making them a feature in themselves. The flower spikes tower above the leaves and are soft mauve and shaped like a funnel, and the flowers are pink and white. Acanthus is one of the few plants whose flowers you do not remove when flowering has finished, because when the seedpods appear they are most decorative.

Acanthus can be difficult to move to a new position or eradicate completely as they have long, thong-like roots that spread underground; therefore choose the planting position carefully. However, don't let this put you off planting them, as they are beautiful garden plants. *A. spinosus* is probably the pick of them, as its leaves are very decorative and divided, and it is very free flowering.

Aconitum

Also known as monkshood, this plant has beautiful spire-like flowers; it also has fibrous, tuberous roots that are poisonous if eaten, but are otherwise harmless. The hooded flowers are usually in shades of blue, but the variety 'Ivorine' is creamy white. There is also a climbing form, *A. volubile*, which is not commonly seen but is a useful climber to scramble through early flowering spring shrubs such as forsythia, syringa and Ribes (flowering currant), all of which have very uninteresting foliage in the summer months. With such a background, its nodding blue flowers cause quite a stir.

A. 'Bressingham Spire' is a very compact plant, with violet-blue flowers carried on a very erect, sturdy spike, so staking is not essential. The flowers rise above dark green leaves, and are very deeply divided and glossy. It is definitely advisable to plant in groups of three or five at the minimum.

All aconitums prefer to be planted out in an open sunny position, but will tolerate light shade.

Alchemillas

Alchemillas are a small family, but form an essential part in any herbaceous scheme, and look well when used as an under-planting or edging to rose beds. They are commonly known as 'lady's mantle' or 'fairy's dewpond'.

All varieties of alchemilla carry delightful sprays of tiny, greenish-yellow flowers. They grow happily in full sun or partial shade, and are completely hardy. As the flowers fade they must be removed as

Acanthus mollis *grows well on clay.*

soon as possible, otherwise they turn a most horrid shade of brown.

The plant forms dense clumps of ground-hugging foliage in the winter. In early spring, stems emerge bearing pale green leaves with crinkled edges; after rain each leaf holds a raindrop in its centre, hence the name 'fairy's dewpond'. Such a beautiful plant deserves several places in even the smallest garden, and this can be achieved by dividing the existing plants in the early spring, or using the self-sown seedlings that appear round the parent plant. *A. mollis* is the most popular plant in this group.

Alstroemeria

The alstroemeria, or Peruvian lily, is a summer-flowering tuberous perennial, with flowers in all colours except blue. They are normally frost hardy, but in the event of a very cold, frosty spell, putting surface mulch over their planting position some 2 to 3in (5 to 8cm) deep would help to protect them. They love being in a sunny position, in a humus-enriched soil.

Ligtu hybrids (*Alstroemeria ligtu*) have mixed colours, and although expensive, are well worth planting. Because of their tuberous root system they are not easy to move around, so their planting position should be selected with care. Also for the same reason they are difficult to eradicate.

Anemones

Common name 'windflowers', this is a very diverse family of bulbs and herbaceous plants, again varying enormously in height and form of leaf shape, and with a very wide colour range. *Anemone x hybrida* syn. *japonica* is a group of very vigorous branching perennials, with rhizomatous roots that travel underground to form additional plantings elsewhere. The leaves are oval shaped, and often divided into several leaflets. They are fully hardy and thrive in full sun or light shade; they do require soil that has been enriched with humus, not only to provide nourishment but also to retain moisture. For pure simplicity and long flowering, the variety 'alba' is one of the best: its pure white flowers with yellow centres seem to go on and on, from late summer well into the autumn.

Aquilegia

Aquilegia, or columbines, are a genus of graceful, clump-forming, short-lived perennials, grown for their very attractive, nodding, bell-shaped, spurred flowers in spring and summer. They prefer an open, sunny site with plenty of humus in the soil, but they are fully hardy, and will stand up well to cold, frosty spells. As they are short-lived, one wonders if it is worth buying expensive named varieties, rather than raising them from seed or buying a box of plants in mixed colours from the nursery or garden centre. Once planted, although the original plants will only survive for two to three seasons, you will find they provide you with a ready supply of attractive self-sown seedlings – often the seedlings are more beautiful when in flower than their parents. Bearing in mind their beauty in the

Astrantia major.

flower borders, it is essential to incorporate them in any scheme. No single named variety of aquilegia has been selected for recommendation here; rather any aquilegia will be worthy of its place in the clay garden.

Astrantia

Astrantia, or masterwort, is a genus of perennials that is fully hardy, but requiring sun or semi-shade. They are clump-forming, and the flowers come in shades of white, white and green, and several shades of pink and maroon. Throughout the summer the foliage is a light green with cut edges. *A. maxima* is a lovely rose-pink form.

Campanula

The name 'campanula' means 'having flowers that are bell-shaped'. This is a genus of spring- and summer-flowering perennials, some of which are evergreen. Hardy, they grow in sun or shade, but the very pale pinks and blues prefer not to be out in the full glare of the sun. They range from alpines, through those that cover the ground, to plants that are 4 to 5ft (1.2 to 1.5m) tall. With such a diversity, it is difficult to select one that towers above the rest, but *C. lactiflora* 'Prichard's Variety' must rate very highly, with its upright stems up to 5ft (1.5m) in height, and carrying branching heads of bell-shaped violet blue flowers, from early summer to late autumn.

Echinacea

Also known as the cone flower, up to a few years ago echinaceas were rarely seen in our gardens, but now they are everywhere, and rightly so. This genus prefers to be grown in full sun in humus-enriched soil, when it will flower all summer. It is an upright perennial, growing up to 4ft (1.2m) in height. Its stems are very sturdy and rarely require staking. The leaves are lance-shaped, dark in colour, and it has large, daisy-shaped flowers. The variety 'Robert Bloom' has deep crimson-pink flowers with a dark brown cone at their centre. Because it is so long flowering, it needs to be continually deadheaded.

Eryngiums

The sea hollies are another group that have gained in popularity in recent years. They can be either perennials or biennials, but in the case of biennials they can be considered to be permanent, as there are always young plants to take over when the parents die. They often have beautiful, marbled foliage, both their basal leaves and up their stems. They are fully hardy, and, as their common name implies, are happy growing by the sea.

E. *giganteum* 'Miss Wilmott's Ghost' is a very striking plant with beautifully marked foliage and large, blue, thistle-like flowers, surrounded by spiny, silvery bracts in late summer. After flowering the plant dies, but this is not a problem as there are numerous young ones to take its place. If you want to transplant any of the young seedlings, do this as soon as they are big enough to handle, because as they mature, it is difficult to accomplish this without damaging their root system. Growing wild on the sea shore, the seedlings have to develop a tap-

Euphorbia characias wulfenii.

root system to go down through the sand or shingle to find nourishment below, and the same root system develops in garden cultivation. E. 'Miss Wilmott's Ghost' looks lovely in twilight or darkness, and is an ideal plant for growing in a night garden, which is becoming a very popular concept.

Euphorbias

Also known as milkweed or spurge, the euphorbias are a very large family of shrubs, succulents and perennials. The shrubby ones fit in well with any herbaceous planting, possibly enhancing it. The flower heads have cup-shaped bracts in various colours, but often limey green, each containing several flowers lacking both petals and sepals. It doesn't mind where it grows, apart from deep shade. When pruning or cutting back, do be careful of the sap that exudes from the wound as this can cause skin irritation.

E. *charracias* subspecies *wulfenii* is an evergreen upright shrub. The stems are biennial, producing grey-green leaves the first year, and in the second year, enormous globular elongated heads, limey green with a red eye. When flowering has finished, cut the stems down to the base.

Left: Geranium *'Johnson's Blue'.*

Below: Helenium *and* Rudbeckia *together make a strong impact.*

Geraniums

There must be a geranium for every position in the garden: they are most accommodating plants, and easy to grow. These are the herbaceous geraniums, not to be confused with the non-hardy 'geraniums' that are used for summer bedding. Because they are so accommodating, they are easy to hybridize so new varieties are coming on to the market all the time. Most of them are semi-evergreen or evergreen, and even more so as we seem to be getting milder winters. Most prefer to be grown in full sun, but some will tolerate semi-shade. They do not like too rich a soil, as this seems to promote more foliage than flower. Some of the newer varieties, such as 'Ann Folkard', which has deep magenta flowers with black veins, and 'Ballerina' with purplish pink and deep purple veins, are excellent free-flowering garden plants. *G. cinereum* var. *subcaulescens*, a spreading variety with round, deeply cut, soft green leaves, is fabulous when used as a foil for silver-leaved plants because it has deep purple magenta flowers with a striking black eye and stamens.

G. endressii 'Wargrave Pink' is an old variety that has rightly stood the test of time, having dense, dainty, lobed leaves and bright, salmon-pink flow-

Mixed hostas.

ers that appear from early summer onwards and look wonderful in association with nepeta, alchemilla and lavender. Probably the most eye-catching of them all is *G. psilostemon*, a clump-forming perennial with deeply divided leaves that take on most beautiful autumn colouring. It is very free-flowering with large, cup-shaped magenta flowers that have a penetrating deep black eye.

Helenium

Helenium is also known as 'sneezeweed'. A few years ago the heleniums lost popularity, which was a shame as they are superb autumn-flowering plants. Fortunately this situation has been reversed. They are grown for their sprays of daisy-like flowers intensified by a brown central disc. Again, they are fully hardy and must have an open sunny position. Their colour range is very autumnal, going through shades of yellow, orange, russets and reds, and they really bring back to life a border that was glorious in the summer but looking tired by autumn.

H. 'Bruno' grows to 4ft (1.2m) tall, and has sturdy stems supporting sprays of deep bronze to red flowers. There are other, older varieties that grow taller, but colour-wise 'Bruno' is one of the best.

Hostas

Also known as 'plaintain lily', hostas are grown mainly for their decorative and striking foliage. They form large clumps that are superb as ground coverers. They are fully hardy and prefer shade, as too much sun can cause the foliage to scorch. They vary in height from a few inches to as much as 4ft (1.2m) and can have a spread of up to 5ft (1.5m). Slug and snail protection is essential as they love hostas.

H. sieboldiana (the blue-leaved hostas in the middle of the picture) has enormous leaves, heart-shaped, deeply ribbed, puckered, and blue-grey in colour. The flowers are pale lilac, and trumpet-shaped. With such a size of leaf and spread it is not necessary to plant more than one in a group, unless the garden is a very big one and it could take clumps of three or five. *H. sieboldiana* makes a superb decorative plant in a container, especially in a north-facing position.

Penstemon

Like echinaceas, penstemons have become very popular in the last few years, and are proving hardier than was thought previously. With the

Iris Sibirica.

possibility of climate change, they may become everyday garden plants. They prefer full sun and a well drained fertile soil. On clay this can be achieved by working in some grit at planting time.

P. 'Garnet' has already proved its garden value over the last few years. It is a vigorous plant, very free-flowering, with very narrow leaves, mid-green in colour. Its deep wine-red flowers appear from mid- to late summer, even into early winter. It is very much a plant that needs its faded flowers constantly removed to keep the succession going. It can grow to 2.5ft (75cm) wide and the same in height, so for once, single specimens are all right in the border. Because of its vigorous growth you may want to reduce its width and height, but this is best carried out every spring because the foliage left on during the winter protects the plant.

Phlox

This is yet another family that supplies plants for many purposes, including alpines and ground coverers, ranging in height from medium to tall. Phlox cover the whole colour spectrum except yellow; many are perfumed, and none more so than the group named *paniculata*. The paniculatas are an essential part of every cottage garden. The stems of highly perfumed flowers come into bloom from midsummer onwards; they are fully hardy and, like the anemones, enjoy being grown on humus-enriched soil.

In midsummer, *P. paniculata* 'Eva Cullum' bears conical heads of clear pink flowers with a magenta eye. Unlike most perennials, it should not be cut down to ground level after flowering, but the faded cone should be removed, and in a short space of time small sprays of flowers will appear all up the stem, emerging from the base of the stem leaves.

Polemonium

Polemonium – also known as Jacob's ladder – is a genus of perennials that flower in late spring to early summer, and like an open situation. The foliage is finely divided, and mid-green in colour; there is also a variegated form.

P. caeruleum is a clump-forming variety, with clusters of cup-shaped, lilac-blue flowers with orange-yellow stamens that open as the stems arise through the foliage.

Salvia

The perennials should not be confused with the red bedding varieties and the herbal sages. They are classified in a sub-group *S. virgata nemorosa*, and are fully hardy, forming neat clumps. Their foliage is oval-shaped, rough-textured, and mid-green in colour. In midsummer the flowers are held on branching stems and come in several shades of blue. *S. n.* 'May Night' has a profusion of violet-blue flowers, and if you keep deadheading, it goes on and on and on! Their neatly formed clumps are a feature in the winter garden.

As regards the cutting down of herbaceous plants, this process is clearly detailed both in this chapter on page 50, and in Chapter 13; so too is the treatment of penstemons (*see* page 58).

Sedum

Sedum, or stonecrop, is a member of the succulent family *Crassulaceae*, as they have very fleshy leaves. They prefer to grow in full sun to give of their best, and grow in any soil, although poorer soil suits them better than soil enriched with humus, as the latter makes them grow vigorously and they then topple over, because the root system is unable to support such a wealth of top growth. Too much nourishment produces growth at the expense of flower production.

Many of them make good rock garden or trough plants, but their best use is as front-of-the-border plants when planted in groups. *S. spectabile* (also known as the 'ice plant') is best for this purpose, especially when planted in groups. It has oval, fleshy, indented, grey-green leaves. Emerging from the leaves come flat heads of tiny star-like flowers, ranging in colour from white, through pink, to red, depending upon the variety chosen. *S. spectabile* 'Brilliant' is a lovely variety, with bright, rose-pink flowers borne in great profusion in the autumn. The flat heads attract bees and butterflies.

Sidalcea

Sidalceas are a perfect substitute for delphiniums, and certainly do not attract slugs and snails in the same way. They require full sun. The variety 'Jimmy Whittet' has bright green divided leaves and delicate, single, purplish pink flowers all the way up its tall spire. There are also some named varieties from Shakespeare's *A Midsummer Night's Dream*, such as Puck and Oberon, coming into the nurseries and garden centres, which might be worth looking out for.

CHAPTER 8

Annuals

Having dealt with trees, shrubs and perennials, it follows that there should be a brief chapter on annuals. Like everything else, there are fashions in gardening that come and go. Thus ferns may be the rage for a few years, and are then rarely mentioned in the gardening press except for suggestions to place them in the dreariest part of the garden. Then suddenly they may be back in favour. Fuchsias' popularity went up and down like a reading on a thermometer, as happened with annuals, which at present are very much 'in vogue'.

Annuals grow quite happily on clay soils, provided the top 6in (15cm) of the soil has been enriched with moisture-retentive compost, as they are not deep-rooting plants. Using them in a new, bare garden is the quickest way to provide a wealth of greenery and flowers. Their other great advantage is that they can be used as in-fillers between shrubs and roses for the first two or three years after these have been planted and while they are becoming established. Maybe you will become so fond of them you will designate a special area for them so they can be used in the garden every year.

PLANTING SCHEMES

Using annuals amongst vegetables can be visually very dramatic, and some of them, Calendula (common name 'marigold') for example, can keep pests and diseases at bay. For instance, rows of carrots and onions both suffer from their own particular type of fly that can cause untold damage, but a row of Nigella (love-in-a-mist) planted between the rows can solve this, and look very decorative at the same time.

Nigella, *otherwise known as love-in-a-mist.*

Annuals in beds and borders or vegetable gardens do not necessarily have to be planted in straight rows. For example they could, in a very small way, replicate the famous fruit and vegetable garden at Villandry in the French Loire region, where they are sown in geometric shapes and patterns – in circles, squares, rectangles and triangles – with fruit, flowers and vegetables all intermingling: so 'over the top', but so fabulous, and in a miniature way you could do it here.

Most annuals have a lightness to their form, so can often bring a touch of softness to adjacent planting, such as the hard, dark green, heavily veined leaves of *Viburnum davidii*. Furthermore, they should not only be thought of as ground-cover plants, but are extremely useful when trained up supports to give a flat area some height, thus changing the appearance of that part of the garden. Sweet peas, *Thunbergia alata* (black-eyed susan) and the genus *Ipomoea* (morning glory) in both the traditional Mediterranean blue and other vibrant colours are just some examples. Climbing nasturtiums do not have to climb, but can be allowed to trail over the ground.

Annuals do not have to be sown in separate groups – two or three kinds can happily be grown together. An example of this is to sow *Calendula* 'Geisha Girl', which is vibrant orange in colour, with the clear blue of Nigella, each complementing the other. Alternatively they can be sown in drifts, or the seed mixed prior to sowing to create a wildflower meadow effect. Like perennials, the more they are deadheaded, the more they go on flowering. If you sow a scheme that is wider than you can reach from any side, a plank of wood supported at each end ensures you can reach and deadhead those in the centre.

SOWING YOUR ANNUALS

Annuals can best be sown directly *in situ* in mid-March or April onwards. They can be sown in pots, but when planted out take a few weeks to establish themselves and grow into each other to achieve the 'natural' look. They vary in height from very low to quite tall, but this can be a visual delight. Cleomes (spider flowers), Statice (sea lavender) and rudbeckias can give exciting height to combined planted borders.

Once you have decided what annuals you want and where they are to go, ensure the site is weed-free and raked level with some pelleted chicken manure scattered over the surface. Then make shallow indentations in the soil and sow the seed into these. After sowing the seed, cover it with soil and water in. On germination, if you have sown too thickly, it may be necessary to thin the seedlings out, so that each one has its own space in which to develop: thin out so there are 3 to 6in (7 to 15cm) between each seedling you want to retain. When this has been done, water in the remaining seedlings to compensate for possible root disturbance.

While there have been dramatic developments in improving varieties, it is still the old varieties such as clarkia, godetia, candytuft, mignonette and night-scented stock that give the English look to the garden.

Many annuals are self-seeders, meaning that the young ones appear each spring to take the place of their parents that died the previous autumn. They may seed beyond their original boundaries, but this can be very attractive in mixed borders.

HALF-HARDY ANNUALS

Half-hardy annuals are the plants we buy from the nursery or garden centre once the risk of frost has passed, and include petunias, nicotiana, geraniums and tagetes. They are one-season plants only, but do provide a quick way to get flowers in the borders. At the end of the summer, remove them and replace with polyanthus, winter-flowering pansies and bulbs to give your garden colour and interest all year round.

Wallflowers and Brompton stocks are useful to go with the polyanthus and pansies because they

A bed of geraniums.

are taller; also they are evergreen, so are extremely useful in pots and containers, as well as supplying some form of support to the taller bulbs in the beds and borders. The wallflowers can be grown in separate colours or mixed. Both 'Persian Carpet' and 'Harlequin' are good mixtures, and both types are highly fragrant, which in wallflowers is a must! Being mixed it is not so easy to combine single-coloured bulbs to go with them.

Quite often the wallflowers and stocks will survive two or three seasons before becoming leggy, when they should be discarded. If you want to keep them for more than one season they must have their faded flowers removed before they go to seed, and they could also have their existing growth reduced by half. Having done this, give them one or two foliar feeds as previously described.

A COTTAGE GARDEN

If you want your garden to have either the old-fashioned look or the cottage garden feel, then annuals sown between the existing planting will achieve this. Clarkia, godetia, calendula, *Nigella Reseda*, *Matthiola* (night-scented stock), hesperis, lunaria and nasturtium are all so easy to grow from seed sown *in situ*; or if you prefer, they can be sown in pots, and planted out when big enough to handle.

As previously mentioned, the so-called 'English

look' is achieved by integrating annuals into our beds and borders, but also by allowing the annuals to become permanent residents in areas of the garden that, either by design or neglect, we allow to become wild. Annual poppies, eschscholzia (Californian poppies) – which come in a fabulous colour range of red, orange, apricot, yellow, cream and white – and sweet rocket (*Hesperis matromalis*), when combined with honesty, cornflowers and wild white daisies, will give you the look you are after.

MOVEABLE STRUCTURES

Obelisks or pyramid structures are very much in vogue at present, and if one or several half wooden beer or wine casks are planted up with a combination of annuals and half-hardy annuals, they can become an important part of any garden scheme. However, before filling the casks with compost, turn them upside down and screw four furniture castors on to each base: this will make them easier to move about. Then fill them with multi-purpose compost to within 1in (2.5cm) of the top, gently firming it as you go. Insert your structure into the centre of the cask.

Having done this, you can sow seeds of sweet pea, climbing nasturtium, black-eyed susan (*Thunbergia alata*) to climb up and provide you with a continuous succession of blooms throughout the summer. At the base of each pyramid, annuals sown *in situ*, and half-hardy annuals purchased at the garden centre can be planted, including those that will trail and hang down over the edge. Having fitted the castors means you can move the filled cask easily about the garden, for example to where you are planning to have an 'event', or to screen a part of the garden that has gone past its best.

PLANNING YOUR GARDEN PLANTING

There is always a problem with annuals, that if you plant them on undernourished ground, they rarely last the season, but if you provide them with too much goodness, they then tend to provide lush foliage at the expense of producing flowers. However, with a little experimentation you will get

Wallflowers planted out in a raised bed.

it right. Most annuals prefer a good summer to be at their best – when the temperature is two or three degrees above the norm suits them. A wet summer will turn them into a sorry state, though with climate change becoming more possible each day, our summers may become less wet.

It is a mistake to use the same annuals or half-hardy annuals each year in the same place just because they did well there last year. Familiarity breeds contempt, and this is certainly very true in this case. Be brave! Experiment with new families and varieties each year, or at least try some new ones to mix in with the established ones.

If you want an occasional dot plant or a statuesque plant, then *Nicotiana sylvestris* is the annual to go for. It is the stateliest of all the tobacco plants, having good-sized, dark green leaves all the way up its 6ft (2m) tall stems. Its long, tubular, white fragrant flowers are almost ghost-like at dusk or as darkness deepens. Because of its vigour it should be given at least 2ft (60cm) of clear planting space all round it. Although it can be used as a dot plant, it does look wonderful when planted in groups of three, five or even seven – and in such a group, imagine how the perfume intensifies!

CHAPTER 9

Bulbs and Corms

Many bulbs and corms thrive on clay soil, naturalizing themselves by seed or producing bulblets; others do not, but maybe if the bulbs are relatively cheap to buy they should be purchased annually, in much the same way that we use bedding plants. Bulbs are so useful, particularly in the small garden, as they take so little of the growing space, but repay their planting by extending dramatically the flowering interest in the garden.

We tend to think mainly of the bulbs that flower in the spring – daffodils, tulips hyacinths, crocus and snowdrops. But a visit to your garden centre in the autumn and spring, where you will see numerous racks of packets of bulbs, beautifully illustrated in colour, with cultivation instructions, will make you realize how many varieties of bulbs there are for your use throughout the year.

Obviously the more your clay soil has been worked and its condition improved, particularly as far as drainage is concerned, the greater the range you can plant. Bulbs and corms are like all living things, in that they do respond to tender loving care; so often this is given when they are first planted, and then we tend to forget them until they reappear the following year, when they only receive a cursory glance until flower buds appear. We presume that at flowering time they will perform as they did the first year after planting, and are surprised when they don't.

MAKING THE MOST OF YOUR BULBS

Ideally, and this applies to all bulbs and corms, if

Snowdrops (Galanthus) *look appealing growing naturalized in grass.*

you don't want to collect the seed or want the bulbs to drop their seed *in situ*, then as soon as they have finished flowering, you should remove their fading flowers. Then you need to water their foliage with a solution of Maxicrop, Seagold, or any other type of seaweed-based fertilizer. To make the foliar feed solution, add one tablespoonful of the fertilizer to a gallon of cold water, stir in five or six drops of washing-up liquid, and water the bulbs' foliage: the washing-up liquid makes the solution stick to the foliage and prevents it being washed off should it rain.

Repeat this again in two weeks time, and two weeks after the second application the foliage can be cut off at ground level. The foliage will have sent the feed down into the bulb, putting the bulb in good heart for the following season, and the removal of the foliage leaves keeps the garden looking neat and tidy, instead of being littered with knotted bunches of leaves and yellowing foliage everywhere. It can be applied to bulbs growing in grass or lawns, so cutting the lawn can be carried out that much sooner. Where bulbs have been *in situ* for several years and are producing relatively few flowers, the above method of treatment can be carried out and the following season you will be surprised how many flowers are produced.

Sometimes bulbs that were planted in the autumn fail to appear the following spring. The reason for this is that either they have rotted away or they have been eaten by rodents. To prevent this happening, before planting them, dip them in a neat solution of methylated spirits, straight in and out. Note: do not smoke while you are doing this! Rodents do not like methylated spirits, so they will not come near the bulbs. Furthermore, methylated spirits also acts as a fungicide.

Tulips are a favourite spring flower.

Having treated the bulb with the meths, do not plant it in an upright position but at an angle of 45 degrees: the reason for this is, when it rains and the rain penetrates the soil, instead of it running down into the centre of the bulb and rotting it, it runs down the side of the bulb causing no damage at all.

Eventually, all bulbs left *in situ* will increase, and will exhaust the soil in which they are growing of existing nutrients. So every third or fifth year the bulbs should be dug up when flowering has finished, divided or separated, and then replanted, either back in the same position or in other places in the garden, having first worked in compost and fertilizer.

Bulbs can be planted in containers to give additional interest, and of course they are invaluable if you want to brighten up hard surfaces that would otherwise be devoid of colour and greenery.

One should always be generous with quantity when planting bulbs in beds and borders and in the lawn. Planting one hundred *Anemone blanda* is far preferable to planting ten, and will give a wonderful display the following year. From a design point of view it is much better to have ten generous groups in a small garden, to twenty to thirty groups each having a maximum of ten bulbs in each group.

It is not the intention of this chapter to give long descriptions of each group of bulbs, as these can be easily obtained from the back of the packet containing the bulbs, or from any good bulb grower's catalogue: but here follows a brief list of bulbs and corms that will do well in your clay garden, given the proper care and attention.

Winter- and Spring-Flowering Bulbs

- Galanthus (snowdrops)
- Eranthis (aconites)
- Cyclamen (hardy)
- Tulips
- Narcissi (daffodils)
- Hyacinths
- Crocus
- Muscari
- Scilla
- Chinodoxa
- Alliums
- *Ipheion uniflorum*
- Leucojum (snowflakes)

Summer- and Autumn-Flowering Bulbs

- Ornithogalum
- Ixia
- *Tulbagia*
- Schizostylis
- Acidanthera
- *Babiana*
- *Tritelia Crocosmia*
- Sparaxis
- *Lilium*
- Camassia

All these are good on clay, but it helps if you add a mixture of half peat and half sand to the hole at planting time. Muscari and Crocosmia rapidly increase themselves underground, so it is vital that you lift these as soon as flowering is finished, and divide and reset them, because even with the aid of foliar feeding, flower production will be drastically reduced. This should be done every two years.

Above left: Crocus bulbs naturalized in grass add a special appeal to a lawn.

Above right: Narcissi in bloom.

Left: A clump of daffodils is always a cheering sight in the spring.

It is amazing how little room a clump of bulbs takes up. They can be planted in every nook and cranny, and can be put at the base of trees and shrubs. When planted in conjunction with shrubs, bear in mind the colour of the foliage of the shrub, and plant bulbs whose flowers will complement it or be a startling contrast to it. For example *Senecio greyi* looks lovely with blue hyacinths coming through, and the red foliage of the smoke bush *Cotinus coggygria* is stunning with either the tulip 'Queen of the Night' or *Frittilaria imperialis* 'Lutea' emerging from it.

CHAPTER 10

Roses

The first plant that automatically comes to mind when thinking what to grow on clay soil is the rose. Roses are subdivided into various groups: climbers, ramblers, shrub roses, English roses, hybrid teas, floribundas and patio roses (although the latter do not necessarily require clay soil).

Although roses grow quite happily on clay soil, they do appreciate and respond to tender loving care. Like most plants, they do not appreciate their roots sitting in water in the winter. Prior to planting, generous quantities of well rotted manure or garden compost, in addition to an application of fertilizer (a combination of fish, blood and bone), should be incorporated with the soil. This treatment should be repeated in the summer and after the first year, again in March or April.

Roses respond very well to foliar feeding, which should be applied at fortnightly intervals from the beginning of May to the end of July. To avoid scorching, the foliar feed should be applied either in the early morning or the evening. Obviously healthy plants are able to cope better with attacks of disease and pests. As it is high in trace elements, a seaweed-based fertilizer is best for the foliar feed; it is advantageous to add five or six drops of washing-up liquid to the spray, as this helps it adhere to the leaves and prevents it from being washed off by rain.

CLIMBING ROSES

Climbing roses are used to cover walls, trellises, pergolas. The really vigorous ones will grow through shrubs. They are all hardy, bearing old rose flowers, and they often repeat well. Climbing roses are divided into six groups:

'Queen of Denmark'.

CLIMBERS FOR CLAY GARDENS

There are numerous varieties listed in books and catalogues, but the following perform superbly on a clay soil:

- 'The Generous Gardener' (pale pink)
- 'Cécile Brunner' (blush pink)
- 'Compassion' (salmon pink-ringed apricot)
- 'New Dawn' (silver blush pink)
- 'Teasing Georgia' (yellow)
- 'Marigold' (bronze yellow)

Climbing bourbons All these are hardy, bearing old rose flowers, and often repeat well.

Climbing English roses Developed by the renowned rose grower David Austen. They combine the fragrance of the old rose with the wide colour range and repeat flowering habit of the modern rose.

Climbing tea roses These have smaller flowers and require a warmish wall.

Climbing noisette roses A very old group with flowers of a delicate beauty, repeating well.

Climbing hybrid teas Simply the climbing version of hybrid tea roses. These should be continually deadheaded, and pruned to about a third from the ground in the dormant period to encourage new growth and to ensure that the flowers are not always at the top of a shoot or stem, but all the way up a stem.

'Malvern Hills'.

Because climbing roses are frequently planted in a fairly dry position – at the base of a wall, for instance – it is imperative that they are given a surface mulch and feed every spring in order to conserve the rain from the previous season as long as possible.

RAMBLING ROSES

Like climbing roses, ramblers are divided into distinct groups: multiflora hybrids, sempervirens hybrids, species ramblers, and wichuraiana hybrids.

Multiflora hybrids As their name implies, these have large clusters of small flowers; compared with other classes, they have a much stiffer growth. After flowering, or after the display of hips has finished, they should be hard pruned.

Sempervirens hybrids Their name implies that they are always green, but this is not entirely true, although the foliage does hang on for a considerable time. These roses have long, slender but graceful, attractive small leaves.

Species ramblers These carry very simple but elegant flowers. They are superb if allowed to scramble over large areas or into trees. Usually they are scented, and they bear clusters of hips after flowering.

Wichuraiana hybrids These have a graceful growing habit with quite large flowers held in elegant sprays. Unlike other classes, they require little pruning as their nature is to climb and scramble through each other's stems.

The best six rambling roses for growing on clay soil are:

'Malvern Hills' A very reliable repeat flowerer, which is unusual for a rambler rose. It carries small, fully double blooms of a soft canary yellow. It has strong but slender growth with shiny foliage and very few thorns, making it ideal for arches and pergolas, and it has the added bonus of lovely fragrance, which will not be missed as one passes under it.

'Frances E. Lester' This rose carries huge bunches of small, single blooms, which are white and tinted blush at the edges of the petals. It is very highly perfumed, and produces orange hips in the autumn.

'Paul's Himalayan Musk' Probably one of the best of all the ramblers, this rose produces stems of as much as 35ft (10.5m) long. The stems carry blush pink flowers, which are also very fragrant.

'Rambling Rector' This rose is aptly named, because it rambles through any support it can find. It is covered in small, creamy-white, semi-double, very fragrant flowers, followed by clusters of small hips that last well into winter.

'Adelaide d'Orleans' This rose is virtually

'Francis E Lester'.

evergreen, carrying small, creamy-white flowers smelling of primroses. It is another ideal climber for arches and pergolas, as the flowers hang down as if to look at those passing beneath.

'Paul Noel' Sometimes labelled 'Paul Transom', this rose flowers profusely and repeats well. The flowers start off salmon pink and fade to a medium pink. The blooms are medium-sized but very full, with an apple fragrance.

Very few rambler roses flower more than once a year, but exceptions are 'Alberiic Barbier', 'Alexander Girault', 'Francois Turanviller', 'Little Rambler', 'Paul Noel'. However, when ramblers do flower they are a magnificent sight, producing an abundance of blooms. They are vigorous growers and are therefore ideal for covering large areas quickly. These are probably the easiest of all roses to prune, because once they have flowered, the stems should be removed at base level. However, if a display of hips is required, do not prune the rose after flowering. If the growth becomes too dense, some stems that have not flowered can also be removed; but this is the exception rather than the norm. Although most varieties only flower once a year, they produce a superb display of autumn and winter hips. They are also superb support for *Clematis viticella*, which is at its best in late summer and autumn.

These roses are the perfect choice for covering unmoveable, unsightly objects, and again, for arches and pergolas. However, select carefully, as there is no point in choosing a rose that grows between 35 and 50ft (10.5 and 15m) and which will be too heavy to be supported by slender arches, trellises or pergolas.

SHRUB ROSES

In the twentieth century, species roses were crossed with the modern bush roses to produce these shrub roses, which form large bushes some 5 to 6ft (1.5 to 2m) in height. Many of them are repeat flowering and provide a spectacular effect. The following are all recommended; and the size to which they can be expected to grow is given for each one.

'Penelope'.

'Bonica'.

'Roseriae de l'Hay' (7 x 7ft/2 x 2m). This is a vigorous, dense shrub with apple green-coloured foliage. The flowers are a magnificent, rich wine purple, and the buds are a feature in themselves, being elongated with a hint of colour at the tip. They are fragrant, and their perfume can be smelled from quite a distance.

'Buff Beauty' (5 x 5ft/1.5 x 1.5m). One of the best of the hybrid musk roses. The flowers are carried in large trusses, usually in a range of delicate colours. 'Buff Beauty' flowers profusely in the summer, and a second and even a third time if it is deadheaded as soon as the flowers fade. This hybrid musk has flowers of warm apricot yellow, and with its rich, dark green foliage, it brings to the garden a sense of the South of France.

'Penelope' (6 x 6ft/1.8 x 1.8m). Yet another of the hybrid musks, this variety cannot be left out of the selection for gardening on clay. It carries large trusses of creamy pink flowers in great abundance. It is a repeat flowerer but if the third flush is not deadheaded it produces a generous display of hips.

'Rosy Cushion' (2ft 6in x 5ft/75cm x 1.5m). One of the lower-growing shrub roses, forming almost a rounded cushion; its flowers are soft pink. It flowers almost continuously throughout the season.

'Cerise Bouquet' (9 x 8ft/2.7 x 2.8m). The characteristics of this rose are quite the opposite from 'Rosy Cushion': it grows tall and with arching stems, has small grey leaves, and clusters of small, semi-double cerise pink flowers with a raspberry fragrance. It flowers in early summer and does not repeat. However, it is such a wonderful sight when in flower that it deserves a significant place in every garden.

'Bonica' (4 x 5ft/0.2 x 1.5m). This is a lovely shrub rose, some with sprays of small rose-pink flowers that repeat well.

ENGLISH ROSES

First introduced in the 1970s, these roses are a cross between old roses, modern hybrid tea roses and floribunda varieties. The flowers are very similar to the old roses, often with numerous small petals, and are noted for their visual

'Golden Celebration'.

appeal and their fragrance. The following are all recommended; as before, the size to which they can be expected to grow is given for each one.

'Harlow Car' (4 x 3ft/1.2m x 90cm). The flowers are rose pink and are medium sized. It is a very bushy rose that is covered in flowers from the ground up. It makes a superb hedge to divide areas of a garden.

'Jubilee Celebration' (4 x 4ft/1.2 x 1.2m). This rose has large domed flowers of rich salmon pink with golden undertones. The flowers are carried well above the foliage and have an unusual lemon and raspberry scent.

'William Shakespeare' (3ft 6in x 4ft 6in/1.05 x 1.2m). Of the English roses, this is probably the best of the crimson ones. The flowers open rich crimson and fade to a rich purple. It has superb fragrance, and it also has an excellent resistance to disease.

'Golden Celebration' (4 x 4ft/1.2 x 1.2m). One of the largest flowered of the English roses, it produces large cups of a rich golden yellow, with a fragrance of wine and strawberries.

'William Shakespeare'.

'Alba Semi'.

Opposite left:
'Velvet Fragrance'.

Opposite right:
'Warm Wishes'.

OLD ROSES

These are the true old roses of early European origin. They flower in the summer only, many carrying a wonderful fragrance. The following are all recommended, and the size to which they can be expected to grow is given for each one.

'Alba Semi Plena' (7 x 5ft/2 x 1.5m). Produces clusters of large, fragrant, flat and almost single milk-white flowers with golden stamens. The hips that follow flowering are red. This rose has grey-green foliage.

'Celsiana' (6 x 4ft/1.8 x 1.2m). Bears flowers of shell pink with golden stamens; it is semi-double, and sweetly scented.

'Charles de Mille' (5 x 4ft/1.8 x 1.2m). This old rose produces large, opulent, crimson flowers that fade to a hint of purple. It is another fragrant variety.

'Queen of Denmark' (5 x 4ft/1.5 x 1.2m). This is one of the finest of all the roses. It produces large, fragrant, beautifully formed, quartered flowers of soft, glowing pink.

R. gallica officinalis (4 x 4ft/1.2 x 1.2m) Commonly known as the 'Apothecary's Rose' or the 'Red Rose of Lancaster', it has large, fragrant, semi-double blooms with gold stamens. It is very free flowering, extremely healthy, tough and reliable.

William Lobb (6 x 6ft/1.8 x 1.8m) A moss rose with dark crimson, very fragrant flowers, which fade to a violet grey carried well on the stems. Because of its height it is a back-of-the-border rose.

HYBRID TEAS

These roses have superb, pointed buds but little or no fragrance. They do not blend well with other plants, and are best in borders of their own.

'Velvet Fragrance' (5ft x 2ft 6in/1.5m x 75cm). This rose is highly fragrant, as its name implies. The flowers are deep velvet crimson, and are backed by large, deep green leaves.

'Paul Shirville' (3 x 3ft/90 x 90cm). This is a very elegant, salmon pink rose with simple dark foliage and a good fragrance.

'Warm Wishes' (2ft 6in x 2ft 6in/75 x 75cm). This rose produces large, fragrant, peach-coral flowers with dark luxurious foliage that sets off the flowers so well. It is almost always in flower during the growing season.

'Just Joey' (3 x 3ft/90 x 90cm). This wonderful and popular rose has copper-orange flowers with tints of deep rose at the tips of the petals. It is free-flowering, and tends to have a sprawling growth. It is an excellent cut flower.

'Elina' (3 x 3ft/90 x 90cm). The flowers are large, a delicate pale primrose yellow, and single with a faint perfume. It is the epitome of a hybrid tea rose.

'Pascali' (3ft 6in x 3ft 6in/1.05 x 1.05cm). This is a beautiful rose with creamy white, well-shaped flowers and some fragrance. The flowers are medium-sized. It is a strong grower and good for cutting, having long, strong stems.

CHAPTER 11

Climbers and Wall Shrubs

Climbers and wall shrubs are an essential part of any garden because they bring the house and boundary walls or fences into the scheme, rather than leaving them in isolation. Because the beds surrounding the house are usually not very wide, you can improve the soil without a great deal of effort – a particular advantage in clay gardens – which makes the planting of these plants and their subsequent growing so much easier.

Wall shrubs play an integral part in the planting round house walls and other buildings associated with it; without wall shrubs the planting can appear very flat. They provide both height and width, particularly if they have character and interest all year round. They do not necessarily require the protection offered by the walls, although for some it is essential. For others the dryness offered by the soil adjacent to the wall is an ideal growing condition.

Shrub and English roses, once they have got their roots down, flourish and produce regular displays of flowers and perfume throughout the summer because, being against a wall and partly enclosed, their fragrance is enhanced. In some cases the plant's foliage, if it is aromatic, is as important as the flowers.

The most important factor to bear in mind when planting against walls or fences is that this is the first area where plants may show stress due to lack of moisture. So every effort must be made to conserve moisture. We often forget that even though rain may have fallen, the base of the wall may not have received any of it due to the gutters above, or the overhang of the roof, particularly if it is thatched.

Clematis montana alba.

PREPARING TO PLANT

Before any planting is undertaken, if the border has been previously planted, remove any of the occupants you don't like or that have passed their sell-by date, and any weeds. If the weeds are perennial, such as couch grass or ground elder, it may be necessary to clear the border completely and then fork it thoroughly, or apply a weed killer; if the weeds are particularly tenacious, a second application may be necessary.

When the border has been cleaned to your satisfaction, then apply and work in a generous application of well-rotted compost. Follow this with a fertilizer, using one that has an immediate effect such as Gromore, and a longer-lasting one such as combined, sterilized fish, blood and bone at the rate of 2oz per yard run, forking the fertilizer in lightly.

On clay soil, the first plant that comes to mind for this situation is the rose. Remember that if a rose has been growing previously in the position in which you wish to plant a new one, you will have to excavate at least two buckets of soil in which the old rose was growing and replace it with two buckets of soil from somewhere else in the garden that has not had roses growing on it before. The reason for this is a condition called rose sickness, which can remain in the soil for many years, inhibiting growth in the newly planted rose.

Roses have their own chapter in this book (*see* page 69), but it is worth considering them as host plants for other plants to scramble through.

CLEMATIS

Clematis is ideal for combining with roses, because apart from their flowers, many of them carry very

Left: Clematis orientalis *'Lemon Peel' looks striking against the dark green foliage of yew.*

Opposite: Blue clematis is a favourite garden climber.

decorative seed heads that last well into the winter and are delightful when covered with hoar frost. When selecting a variety, you have to decide whether you want it to flower at the same time as the rose, or at a separate time to extend the flowering period. If it is to flower at the same time as the rose, it must complement it and not clash with it, or be so similar in colour that it is hardly visible!

Blue-coloured clematis goes well with yellow or pink roses, but again, ensure that the blue is the right shade to go with the pink. White roses are very complementary to all colours. Red and orange and the various shades of apricot look fabulous with purple and mauve scrambling through.

Clematis flowers vary in size, and the large ones – the size of saucers – can only be used with full blown roses such as 'Compassion' or 'Mme G. Stachlein'. The medium-sized clematis, such as 'Hagley Hybrid' and 'William Kennet' and any variety of the *'viticella'* group, are much better.

Clematis species are normally far too rampant for the average rose, but the Himalayan group such as 'Kiftsgate', 'Rambling Rector' and 'Seagull' can take *C. montana*, *C. flammula* and *C. cirrhosa* with ease, and when planted in this way are a magnificent sight in the garden.

Planting Clematis

Clematis is best planted in the autumn (that is, in September to October), while the soil is still warm and their roots can get a hold before the onset of winter. Clematis planted in the spring often die as their roots have had no chance to establish themselves before being assailed by the possibility of unexpected devastating winds. They are usually pot-grown, so prior to planting, gently tease out the roots at the base, as this helps them to quickly establish themselves into their new surroundings. When planting, once you have excavated the planting hole, work in a generous quantity of coarse grit as this gives added drainage, and also some well-rotted compost. If you have not planted them using the newspaper method (*see* Chapter 3, page 26), then they must be kept well watered through their first growing season.

Potential Problems with Clematis

Clematis suffers from two diseases: mildew, which can easily be controlled by one or two applications of a fungicide, and clematis wilt. Overnight a healthy plant will suddenly collapse and its foliage go black/brown for no apparent reason. This is easily cured, however: cut all the stems to ground level, then give the plant a bucket of cold water, followed by a second bucketful of cold water to which has been added a tablespoonful of Jeyes disinfectant. When new growth appears, allow it to reach 18in (45cm), then cut the growth back to 9in (23cm), and as before, apply the bucket of cold water and a second bucket containing the Jeyes fluid. When this has been completed, no further problems will arise, and the plant will grow normally.

WISTARIA

This is a marvellous climbing plant, and with age it develops the most wonderful twisted and gnarled stems. In May and June it is covered with long, pendant trusses of blue flowers, often highly perfumed. There are several Japanese hybrids that bear white or pinkish flowers, but these seem to go shabby as they age; so for pure perfection, stay with the blues.

Once established, wistarias are vigorous growers and require pruning twice a year, once in July after flowering has finished, and again in November. On each occasion, shorten the secondary side growths back, as this increases flower production the following year. To give added interest, just as the clematis can be planted successfully with the rose, the wistaria can be joined in the same hole with the golden hop, *Humulus aureus*. This herbaceous plant is cut down to ground level every autumn. It has rough, brownish hairy stems that carry yellow-lobed leaves and greenish pendant flower trusses in the summer and autumn. The combination of the yellow leaves and the blue flowers in the early summer is truly stunning.

JASMINES

One of the joys of looking at the garden in the winter months is to see the bright yellow flowers of the winter jasmine, *Jasminum nudiflorum*, appearing from early November through till the end of February or later. It is a deciduous climber, having an arching habit with very dark green leaves that are a perfect backdrop to the bright yellow flowers. Once the *jasminum* has finished flowering, the stems that have borne the flowers should be pruned hard back. This superb climber should be planted in every garden that has clay soil.

There are several other jasmines, but not all of them will thrive on clay, no matter how much the soil is improved. The following will grow successfully on clay:

Jasminum beesianum: This climber can be evergreen or deciduous, depending upon the coldness of the winter, but if it drops its leaves it will soon have new ones when spring starts. In the summer it carries fragrant tubular flowers that are pinkish red in colour. In the early autumn shiny black berries are produced. It should be pruned in the spring when you think the warm weather has arrived.

Jasminum officinale: The common jasmine is semi-evergreen. It has twisted stems, and the white, very fragrant flowers are produced throughout the summer, sometimes extending into the autumn.

Jasminum polyanthum: This is very similar to *officinale* in habit and flowering time.

All the jasmines are vigorous growers and respond to an annual spring feed and mulch.

LONICERA (HONEYSUCKLE)

Although renowned for their perfume, honeysuckles are not the easiest plants to grow on clay soil, since clay is prone to drying out, leaving them short of moisture and therefore under stress; this leaves them very vulnerable to attacks of mildew and attack by aphids, and if damaged in this way they will look very unsightly. This situation can be made even worse if runner beans, peas or any other members of the legume family are growing in the garden. Honeysuckles will grow in full sun but will tolerate some shade.

Of all the honeysuckles, *L. americana* is one of the best to try on clay. It is very free-flowering, carrying clusters of strongly fragrant yellow flowers flushed with red purple staining in the summer; it has a second flush of flowers in the autumn, though not so profuse. It is deciduous. A fairly new hybrid, *L.* 'Graham Thomas', has oval-shaped green leaves that are bluish underneath, showing off the fragrant white flowers perfectly; as the flowers fade they turn to a very clear yellow. It has a very long flowering period in the summer, and is deciduous.

Wistaria brachybotrys *'Alba' grows well against a wall.*

HYDRANGEA

Hydrangea petiolaris is an excellent plant for growing against north walls and other shady positions. It has delightful skeletonized stems, which are a feature in themselves in the winter months, and the stems have hairy sucker pads so the plant is self-clinging to the wall. It has toothed green leaves, and lacy heads of white flowers in early summer. It takes a while to establish itself – young plants produce only a few flowers – but once established, it flowers profusely. It is a good host plant, when established, for any variety of *Clematis viticella.*

The hydrangea looks excellent planted at the base of, for example, an old oak tree, because as it grows upwards it shows through the branches in the summer. Its white flowers are a superb sight, with the added bonus of the leaves turning lemon yellow before they tumble to the ground in the autumn. It can also be trained to grow along, say, the hand rail of a bridge going over a pond, where its flowers are reflected in the water below; or along the top of a low garden wall, where its flowers and autumn colour are looked down on.

Hydrangeas must be kept well watered for the first two or three growing seasons.

SOLANUM

Solanum jasminoides 'Album' is a delightful semi-evergreen climber, a member of the potato family, which is very evident when you see its flowers. It is a fast-growing, woody climber, with lance-like shaped leaves, and star-shaped white flowers, sadly not perfumed; however, as if to compensate for this, it starts flowering in late spring and continues well into the autumn. This is an ideal subject to grow together with another climber, and also perfect for a pot or other type of container.

PARTHENOCISSUS

This group of plants is commonly known as 'Virginia creeper', and grows best on north or east walls. They are all deciduous, having woody stems with far-reaching tendrils, the tips of which have sucker pads, making them self-clinging. They may take one or two years to establish themselves, but they can become rampant, which is an admirable quality where there is a large, high wall that needs to be covered. They do well climbing up established trees, but remember to plant them against the shadier side of the tree.

P. henryana has long velvety leaves, deep green to bronze, with either white or pink pronounced veins. Like all parthenocissus, the flowers are insignificant, green in colour, but they do produce dark blue-black berries in clusters.

P. quinquefolia has rather drab leaves, five-lobed and toothed in shape and dull green in colour, but they turn the most brilliant crimson in the autumn, becoming a real show stopper.

P. tricuspidata, commonly known as Boston ivy or Japanese ivy, is a vigorous climber with spectacular crimson autumn leaf colour.

All the parthenocissus are very easy plants to grow. They are relatively trouble free and easy to grow on clay soils.

VITIS

Vitis (vines) prefer full sun or semi shade. They all have woody stems with tendrils. The ornamental ones grown as climbers bear tiny black fruits as opposed to grapes.

Vitis vinifera 'Brant' is fully hardy, with leaves that are lobed and toothed in shape and bright green in colour, turning brown-red in October. This plant is probably better than *V. coignetiae* for restricted areas.

Vitis coignetiae (otherwise known as the 'crimson glory vine') is very vigorous, reaching up to 60ft (18m) with no problem; it is excellent for growing up trees and covering unsightly walls and buildings. Its large leaves can be anywhere between 10 and 12in (25 and 30cm) in length,

and 6 to 8in (15 to 20cm) across at the widest point. The leaves have a paler under-surface which is also hairy; in the autumn they turn the most fantastic colours, from orange to red to brilliant crimson.

Vitis vinifera 'Purpurea' has three- or five-lobed leaves, purplish in colour with a silvery underside throughout the summer, so this is not a vine that will provide autumn colour. However, it makes a superb backdrop to pink roses and blue clematis when growing up and through a pergola. It can be planted to scramble through an established *Pyrus salicifolia pendula* (weeping silver-leaved pear tree) or *Elaegnus angustifolia*, a large, deciduous shrub with very narrow silvery leaves and tiny yellow fragrant flowers in early summer – an example of two plants growing side by side and complementary to each other.

SUPPORTING CLIMBERS

Shrubs that need to grow against the wall include *Feijoa sellowiana*, *Buddleia crispa*, *Aloysia triphylla*, *Carpenteria californica*, any variety of Myrtus (myrtle), and any variety of Pittosporum, which with shelter offered by the walls, can form naturally large cylindrical towers with either green or variegated foliage.

If the wall is not interrupted by too many windows, then nothing is more majestic than having *Magnolia grandiflora* and its many varieties growing against it. *Azara microphylla* is a much underrated wall shrub, possibly because of its insignificant foliage, but when it is in flower in the early spring, its perfume fills the air for some considerable distance. *Cytisus battandieri* will grow out in the open, but if trained to grow up a wall, this Moroccan broom with its evergreen, silky, silvery-grey leaves and its pineapple-scented yellow flowers that appear for a long period from late spring onwards, is a must. It is a fast grower, so other than the leaders, it needs to be pruned hard back when flowering has finished.

Solanum crispum 'Glasnevin' is, like the cytisus, a fast grower; it has blue flowers with golden eyes, and should be pruned in the same way. Its relation *S. jasminoides* is much smaller and neater in habit,

HEALTH AND SAFETY

A word of caution: if you are doing the work of fixing supports on a wall yourself, ensure you have somebody at the base of the ladder to steady it while you are working on it. If the surface on which the ladder is to stand is uneven, place it on a soft mat or similar material, and it will find its own even level. Do not lean out to reach something which is not within easy reach; it is better to move the ladder so you can do it in comfort. There are now on the market reasonably priced moveable platforms on wheels that may be a better option than a ladder, and such platforms have innumerable uses in the garden.

very free-flowering, with delicate-looking white flowers, again with a golden eye.

Wall-climbing plants, with the exception of self-clinging ones, will require some sort of support to keep them against the wall. The best method is to fix horizontal wires going across the wall, held in place by 'vine eyes'. These are screws that go into the wall and have rings at their tops, through which strong metal wire is threaded. It is possible to put up all the lines in one go, but as it may take the plants several years to reach the top it may be better to fix up additional rows as they are required. The rows should always be put up at the same distance apart, such as 12in, 15in or 18in (30cm, 38cm or 45cm).

Wall Shrubs to Choose

Shrubs that look good with walls as a background but do not necessarily need their protection include all the following: *Choisya ternata*, *Viburnum tinus*, *V. carlesii*, *V. carcephalum*, *Abutilon vitifolium* and its variety 'Album', *Abelia grandiflorum*, *Garrya elliptica* (particularly good in a north-facing situation), *Daphne 'burkwoodii'*, *D. retusa*, the Hebe family, all the Ceanothus (remember that those varieties with the smallest leaves are the hardiest), Escallonias, Cistus, *Convolvulus cneorum*, and the rosemarys, lavenders and the salvias, particularly the sages with their aromatic leaves.

BASE PLANTING

To bring all this together you need base planting. This can be of several different plants, but for a look of complete simplicity, particularly if the house or cottage is a feature in itself, a planting of Epimediums, hostas and hellebores, with spring bulbs coming through, is all that is required. Do not use daffodils: when they are in flower they are very beautiful, but once they have finished flowering their foliage tends to be very messy and lasts for a considerable time.

If you want a mixed base planting then select from the following:

- Hebes
- Potentillas
- Daphnes
- Salvias (the dwarf shrubby sages)
- Ballota
- Euphorbias (again, the dwarf varieties)
- Penstemons
- Hemerocallis

CHAPTER 12

Vegetables, Herbs and Fruit

We tend to think of fruit and vegetable growing as being of practical use only, but with all the new varieties coming in, with larger, more brightly coloured flowers, multi-coloured pods and very diverse foliage, they can become a very decorative part of the garden. They can be combined with step-over fruit trees to line the path edges, or cordon or espalier fruit trees; obelisks and climbing frames can be used to support climbing peas, beans, cucumbers and gourds; beds can have a central feature of a standard gooseberry or some other soft fruit, or bring in a standard bay or rosemary, so that the idea of herbs comes into the scheme. A standard honeysuckle would not look out of place either; these catch the eye not only in the growing season but in the dormant period as well. Wherever possible introduce plants that have evergreen foliage to the winter scene, such as curly kale, and the rounded shapes and coloured leaves are very useful.

Fruit, vegetables and herbs will generally grow happily on clay soil, provided some initial preparation is carried out. Quite often on clay soil that hasn't been cultivated before, potatoes are planted to create a more workable soil. However, it would be advisable before planting to apply one or two applications of Claybreaker, obtainable from garden centres, combined with generous quantities of good moisture-retaining compost and grit to improve the drainage.

Raised beds make excellent places in which to grow your herbs and vegetables; certainly they are a perfect solution to growing shallow-rooted crops such as lettuce, radish and spring onions. Another

Growing your own vegetables is one the most rewarding aspects of being a gardener.

idea is to incorporate them into your beds and borders: using them in this way gives the garden a cottage garden feel. Use climbing supports.

No two clay gardens are the same: the intensity of the clay may vary, and the situation certainly will, from being very exposed to one that is sheltered, either due to natural surroundings or to man's intervention by putting up shelter belts or fences or walls. It is only by keeping trying that you will learn what you can get from your clay soil. There is nothing like the thrill of eating something that you have produced yourself.

VEGETABLES IN THE CLAY GARDEN

One of the easiest vegetables to grow on clay is the potato. People who do not want to grow vegetables on a permanent basis, often plant potatoes in the first year, as not only do they thrive on clay, producing good crops, but at the same time potatoes, even in one year, help to break down the clods of soil into more manageable pieces.

Potatoes come in four groups: early, main, late and salad. Of the earlies, Sharpes Express has to be the front runner, with its beautiful waxy golden skin and its fabulous flavour. Other earlies include Maris B. and Foremost. Wilja, Pentland Squire and Kestrel are the best of the newer main crop varieties. King Edward and Majestic are still two of the best late ones. In recent years Pink Fir Apple has sprung to the front of the salad varieties, with Charlotte and Belle de Fontenay close behind.

Provided the clay soil has been broken down into a reasonable tilth and enriched with both humus and fertilizer, the growing of salad crops should not be a problem. As stated earlier in the book, sow only

A raised vegetable garden.

a portion of the seed in the packet. Sowing the entire content of a package in one go can produce a bumper crop well beyond the consumption requirements of an average family: who wants two hundred lettuce or four hundred radishes all ready at the same time?

As with the salad crops, if the soil has been prepared well, and is in a reasonably well-drained condition, there is no reason why onions and shallots should not be cultivated. As with the broad bean Aquadulce, overwintering Japanese onions can be tried, as they will give you a very welcome crop in early summer.

A word of advice: onions and shallots benefit from being immersed straight in and out of a bowl of neat methylated spirits. Birds do not like its smell, so are less inclined to pull the newly planted sets out of the ground, and it seems to act as a fungicide, helping to prevent basal rot.

The varieties of peas and beans listed here are only the tip of the iceberg, and there are many other varieties worth trying. The recent years of intensive breeding have led to yellow, purple, striped and spotted beans, all of which give visual pleasure both out in the garden and on the plate.

The important thing to remember, particularly with beans, is never to let them get too old: if you break one in half and it doesn't leave a clean break or tries to hang together, it's too old to eat

VEGETABLES TO GROW ON CLAY

The best vegetable varieties for growing on clay are:

- Spring (salad) onions: White Lisbon, Ishikuro and Perfomer
- Spinach: perpetual and Scenic Oriento
- Swiss chard, especially its white variety Lucullus
- Lettuce: Red Salad Bowl, Mini Green and Webbs Wonderful
- Beetroot: Detroit, Golden Globe, Crimson Globe and Bolt Hardy
- Parsnips: Gladiator, Albion and the old variety Tender and True
- Carrots: Infinity, Rainbow and again, another old variety, Early Nantes
- Broad bean: Bunyards exhibition and Masterpiece (and one to sow in the late autumn to give you an early crop: Aquadulce)
- Peas: Kelvedon Wonder, Hurst Green Shaft
- Climbing beans: Blauhilde, Fasold and Goldfield
- Runner beans: Scarlet Emperor, an old favourite, Polestar and Whiteladies.

Left: A well-cultivated vegetable garden.

Below: Salvia officinalis purpurea.

and should be put on the compost heap, as it will be way past its best!

At the end of the growing season, never dig the plants up, but cut the stalks off at ground level, putting these on the compost heap, leaving the root balls in the ground to decay, as these contain numerous nitrogenous nodules, which as they decay enrich the surrounding soil.

HERBS

Room should always be found in the vegetable garden or surrounding borders to grow herbs. It is essential to provide good drainage in an open, sunny position, and then their growing should not be a problem. Plantings of aromatic herbs along the path edges not only provide perfume, but are also very tactile: rosemary, thyme, lavender and teucrium are perfect plants for this. Clumps of chives planted in the corners of each bed, with their lovely green growths and attractive flower heads, provide useful garnishes for salads and cooking in general. They also have the added advantage of deterring many undesirable insects from entering the area, and keep some diseases at bay, such as blackspot.

Cherry in blossom.

The two most difficult herbs to grow in your clay garden will be tarragon and basil, and it may be advisable to plant these in pots in well drained compost, and then plunge the pots up to their necks in the ground. The various varieties of mint should also be planted and plunged in this way, not to assist their growth but rather to restrict their invasive root system.

Coriander, dill, chives, parsley, oregano, marjoram, mint, thyme and rosemary should all be included, and should be picked on a regular basis so that at all times you are picking young growth.

Sorrel is a very underrated plant that enjoys growing on clay; its foliage adds a certain piquancy to so many dishes, and is wonderful combined with watercress to make a soup. Even on the driest winter's day its spear-like foliage is crying out to be picked – and once picked it seems to be replaced immediately by another leaf.

FRUIT

Like vegetables and herbs, most people like to grow some fruit even in the tiniest garden, or possibly in containers: the growing of all these is very therapeutic, and it is so satisfying to think that what you have eaten you have also grown! Possibly a blackcurrant bush, a gooseberry bush and a few strawberries may be all you have room for, but do grow them.

Fruit Trees

Top fruit – apples, plums and pears – all do well on clay soil, provided it doesn't get waterlogged: if this happens it can lead to an attack of canker, which will eventually cause the death of the tree.

Fruit trees do not have to take up a lot of room, as they come ready trained from the nursery as espaliers, cordon and 'step-over' trees. Step-over trees have only two horizontally trained branches,

Cordon-trained fruit trees.

and are used as an edging to a vegetable garden. Because the sap flows horizontally and not upwards, it is restricted, causing fruit buds rather than growth buds to form. They are very productive. As their name implies, you can step over them to reach the beds and borders because their maximum height is never more than 20in (50cm).

With normal fruit trees it is advisable to plant those that are worked on a dwarfing stock, because even in a large garden it makes it easier to prune, spray and pick the fruit, as the trees only reach about 10ft (3m) tall. At this height they also allow maximum light to penetrate all parts of the garden. Whereas a very tall Bramley apple tree casts a lot of shade and is difficult to maintain, it does have the

advantage of providing somewhere cool to sit under its branches on a very hot summer's day, and also looks wonderful in bloom in the spring, and in the autumn when it is full of reddish-green fruits.

Morrello cherries can be purchased as espalier trees, which provide an abundance of fruit when planted against a north-facing wall. It is vital that you net them before the fruit is ripe, because if you don't, the blackbirds will have the lot! The cherries make lovely jam and jellies. Peaches, nectarines and apricots, particularly with our growing seasons getting warmer, do well on south- or west-facing walls. Peach Rochester and apricot North Park hybrid will grow and fruit as free-standing trees.

If it is your intention to remain in your property

for a long time, consider planting a mulberry tree sooner rather than later, because mulberry trees take many years to bear fruit.

Soft Fruits

The soft fruits – strawberries, raspberries, loganberries, black-, white- and redcurrants, and gooseberries – all do well on clay soil, and some even prefer it. The strawberries and raspberries will require an annual application of humus-enriched compost worked in, and also a spring mulch. All, apart from the strawberries, are permanent residents of the garden. The strawberries will have to be replaced every third or fourth season, but as they produce runners, these can be used as the new plants. Red- and whitecurrants and gooseberries make excellent mini- or half-standard trees, and can be used as the focal point in a formal vegetable garden scheme, thus extending their growing area.

Raspberries

Probably of all the soft fruit, raspberries are the best value in the garden, as they are extremely productive and require very little maintenance. There are two separate groups, the summer fruiting and the autumn fruiting, and they are treated in different ways.

Summer Fruiting: These should be planted in the dormant period, November to February. In March the canes are pruned back hard. In a short period new growths will appear, but these will not produce fruit until the following year. Ideally they are trained vertically upright along three or four horizontal wires supported on upright, sturdy poles. The canes should be thinned to 10in (25cm) apart. They fruit any time from June to August, depending on the variety chosen. After fruiting, the canes that have borne fruit should be pruned to just above ground level. At the same time the new canes that have emerged in the spring and summer should, as above, be thinned to 10in apart. This process is repeated on an annual basis for many years, because they can fruit well if properly treated for up to thirty years. Any variety of Malling raspberries, which are the summer ones, are recommended to grow on clay soil.

Autumn Fruiting: Autumn raspberries are trained in the same way, but are pruned at a different time. All growth from the previous autumn and winter is pruned hard back in the spring. New growth will appear very quickly, and this growth will bear fruit in the autumn. They can be thinned to 10in (25cm) apart, or even left as they are.

Raspberries are not deep-rooted, so it is imperative that they are given a generous mulch of well-rotted compost or spent mushroom compost, combined with a granular fertilizer, each spring. They should be kept free of weeds between the plants or in the walkways between the rows, as weeds will find this an ideal medium in which to grow. Both summer and autumn raspberries have yellow fruiting varieties. These are not so prolific in the amount of fruit they produce, but are very decorative on their own or mixed with the red ones.

If you have a good cropping year and you have a surplus, raspberries will freeze very well. Make sure the fruit is dry before putting it into the freezer, otherwise the result will be mushy.

Strawberries

Size is important when selecting varieties of strawberries. The varieties that come from Germany do not have the flavour you might expect, so always select the smaller fruiting ones. Like raspberries, they enjoy regular feeding. They can suffer from attack by red spider mites. If they had a surface mulch of straw on top of the compost mulch to keep the fruit clean, this straw, when it is dry, can be set alight at the end of the growing season. It will burn the leaves carrying the mites, but not the growing crowns.

Strawberries do not freeze well but, like raspberries, can be turned into jam.

Alpine strawberries (*frais du bois*) should be grown in every garden. They can be grown from seed or runners. They have the habit of popping up everywhere in beds and borders, not where you originally intended them to be, but this is part of their charm – so don't be surprised if they emerge in cracks in paving or at the base of steps. One of the pleasures of gardening is to get up in the morning and wander the garden and pick a small bowl of *frais du bois* to have with your breakfast cereal. They

Strawberries do well on clay soil.

fruit over a very long period, often for seven months of the year, with minimum attention.

Loganberries and Tayberries
Loganberries have been about for many years, but tayberries are a recently developed fruit, as are thornless blackberries. These three are all excellent croppers, and make very architectural specimens when fan-trained against a wall or fence. As with raspberries, the canes that have fruited are removed in the autumn, and replacement canes tied in.

Other Fruits

With the seasons becoming warmer, figs will be even more worthwhile growing than they are now. Some seasons, particularly when wet, can be disappointing as regards crops. It will also be possible to grow figs as free-standing small trees, rather than against a wall, as their foliage and grey, naked bark are features in themselves. Of course, if the summers continue to get warmer, in the not-too-distant future oranges, lemons, limes and grapefruits will be grown in many gardens where previously the climate would not have been favourable for such fruits. This observation already applies to olives. Olives have no trouble growing on clay soil, provided plenty of compost is worked well into the soil at planting time, and they are mulched and fed annually. They have very decorative silver foliage, and make a change from *Pyrus salicifolia pendula* (the silver-leaved weeping pear), which can become too vigorous for the smaller garden.

CHAPTER 13

The Four Seasons

CLAY GARDENING IN THE PAST

Until the 1970s people who owned gardens with clay soil only gardened six months of the year: 1 October seemed to be the cut-off date, and apart from picking sprouts on the dishevelled plants in the vegetable garden, that was that until the following Easter. The clay soil became unworkable due to the winter rains, frost and fairly frequent falls of snow. With so much moisture in the ground it became, as described right at the beginning of this book, just like yellow plasticine. The daylight hours were getting shorter, and the desire to go out into the garden in such a miserable environment was not conducive to gardening.

It was always hoped that by 1 March the following year, the days would be starting to get lighter, there would be a hint of warmth in the sun, and new growth would be emerging from the trees, shrubs and perennials. The bulbs, if they had survived growing in such wet conditions, were pushing up the first of, it was to be hoped, many flower buds.

Easter also seemed to be the time when one ventured out into the garden to see what had survived and what had been lost. Lawn mowers were got out to give the lawn its first mow of the season, and possibly some edging and weeding done, fitting in with the family's desire to make excursions into the newly awakening countryside, possibly taking a picnic with them.

The bright berries of Cotoneaster *'Cornubia' brighten up the garden in autumn.*

CLAY GARDENING IN THE PRESENT

Forty years on, how things have changed! Due partly to warming weather, cold, wet days and snowfalls are not such a problem any longer. Gardening programmes on television are more frequent and start earlier in the year. To spur us on to get going, gardening books are given as Christmas presents instead of a pair of socks. There are even a few gardens open under the National Gardens Scheme during the winter. One of these in Gloucestershire promises us that when we have made a tour of the garden, afternoon tea will be served in front of a blazing log fire! Who could resist such an invitation?

It is only when visiting these gardens that one realizes just how much colour and fragrance is about at this time of the year. Fragrance is very important, as it attracts the few pollinating insects about to do their work. Garden centres and nurseries have added to this by highlighting each week or fortnightly what plants are flowering. As these are containerized, they can be taken home and planted straight away.

Tools that at one time were heavy to handle, are now light and made of stainless steel, so as you work the sometimes heavy soil it slides off the blade or the tine rather than adhering to it.

There are many kinds of planting compost and drainage grit available now, which, if incorporated into the planting position, will make the actual planting procedure a pleasure, not a chore. And even in the smallest garden or courtyard, space can be found to plant pots of dwarf bulbs, such as snowdrops, aconites, *Anemone blanda* and the dwarf iris. The use of evergreen trees and shrubs provides a backdrop to these bulbs and to the deciduous early flowering plants.

The summer months can prove just as difficult, with their hot, dry periods and lack of rain, causing the clay soil to crack in numerous places. The cracks are sometimes wide enough to put your hand into them. How do you garden like this? In the seventies you gave up. Now, particularly in the last thirty years, we have learned to live with the soil, learned how to help it come through these difficult periods. Science has advanced enormously, and we now have available soil conditioners, methods of moisture retention, and improved pest and disease control – providing we get the timing right, which we are not always good at.

This chapter is divided into four sections: winter, spring, summer and autumn. Each section deals not only with the management of the garden, but also looks at what should be in flower, and the produce that can be harvested. The four seasons fall into the following sequence: December, January and February are the winter months; March, April and May become spring; continuing to summer in June, July and August; with autumn in September, October and November.

WINTER

Winter is the first of the four seasons to be dealt with, and as already mentioned, predictably, the weather will be warmer than in earlier years. So much have we advanced that people now have winter gardens outside, some big, some small. Cambridge Botanic Garden has a superb winter garden available for the public to see, and although it may be on a far grander scale than you, as the everyday gardener, would ever contemplate undertaking, nevertheless you could use one or more parts of it for inspiration.

Winter-flowering plants are often planted near the house, so they can be seen from the various rooms of the house without having to go outside if the weather should be inclement. To see the purple fragrant-scented *Daphne mezereum* surrounded by yellow aconites and snowdrops or the early flowering crocus, is very exciting and makes you feel spring is on its way. But before considering any new planting ideas, we must get down to basics. If

it hasn't already been done in the autumn, the garden must be tidied. With the advent of winter rains and winds, the first task is to remove rubbish, fallen twigs and branches, fallen leaves, and diseased and dying foliage, particularly in the vegetable garden. If it is left, mild areas previously cleaned of weeds may show signs of more emerging, such as groundsel, poppa cress and willow herb, and if these are not removed now, you will regret it when you see a proliferation of their offspring in the spring.

The Lawn and Landscaping

Even up to Christmas, provided it is still mild, lawns can be mown, which makes the garden look tidy for the festive season, and reduces the amount of grass that has to be taken off in the first spring mowing.

Having mown in December, do remember to send your mower, edging shears and shears to have their winter overhaul before the year is out. So many people delay doing this until just before they need to use them in the spring, and are surprised to find they have to join a queue of like-minded people and have to wait several weeks for their return, by which time the grass could be becoming a bit of a problem.

All the hard landscaped areas such as drives, paths and decking should be cleared of weeds, and if moss or slime is present, a solution of path cleaner available from DIY stores should be applied to prevent them becoming slippery.

Pruning

Provided there is no frost on the plants, or any forecast of frost, pruning can be carried out on most deciduous plants (those plants that drop their leaves in the autumn); ideally evergreens should be left till the spring. Most hybrid tea and floribunda roses can have their previous season's growth shortened by a third. Shrub and Old English roses should have been pruned as their flowering season finished. Buddleias and lavateras will appreciate a similar shortening, even down to half way, as this prevents the wind rocking the taller growth about, causing root disturbance.

Shrubs such as philadelphus, deutzia and

weigelia should also have been pruned as their flowering finished, but if this wasn't done, don't be afraid to do it now – better late than never. Remove stems that show evidence of faded flowers, down to a healthy, tawny brown stem, which will produce the flowers in the coming summer. Even if they have been pruned, with the shrub free of leaves, now is the time to remove crossing or mis-shapen branches.

Remove any suckers at the base of grafted plants. Do not cut them off with secateurs, but pull downwards with your hands, ripping them off, thus preventing new suckers appearing.

Perennial plants, with the exception of iris, peony and penstemon, should have been cut down to ground level after their final flowering – and if this hasn't been done, do it now. Failure to do this gives woodlice, earwigs and other nasties somewhere to hide over the winter. The dying stalks also provide a resting place for fungi to overwinter, before casting their spores to reinfect the borders in the spring.

Fertilizers

Ideally, the garden will have had generous quantities of humus worked into the soil over the previous years. If this is not the case, or if the garden is a new one, when humus becomes available, work it in or at least apply it as a surface mulch. Don't wait till planting time. At planting time also work in additional humus with added grit to any planting that is undertaken at this time of the year. Now is not the time to apply any fast-acting fertilizer: its application leads to the promotion of fast new growth, which the plants' roots would find hard to support, and the new soft growth could be damaged by frost.

Rather, apply a slow-acting fertilizer such as sterilized fish, blood and bone or chicken manure pellets. Both of these are readily obtainable from garden centres or nurseries. Apply at one handful to the square yard or metre.

Plants

So many plants do not survive winter planting – but they should. However, it isn't always the gardener's

Using long-handled pruners to reach high branches.

fault if they don't, because bulbs start appearing in the garden centres from mid-August onwards. As the outside temperature drops, the heating is turned on in the building for the comfort of the customer – but warmth does not benefit the bulbs, which may begin to dehydrate – and once this process starts, there is no going back. The answer is, if you want to buy bulbs that will give a good display at flowering time, buy them as soon as you see them, and then store them in a cool, dry place – or buy direct from a bulb supplier.

Before the arrival of container plants, the majority of plants were supplied by growers from mid-October onwards; the customer had no control over what happened to them at the nursery before they were despatched to him. Once lifted, the roots might have been exposed to the elements, allowing them to dry out before being taken to the packing shed. How long did they lie there before being packed, and then how long were they in transit before arriving at the customer's door? And if the weather was inclement, how long before they were planted? It is not surprising there were so many casualties.

That is not to say that plants supplied from the open ground are a thing of the past. Certainly trees and some shrubs have a better root system if supplied from open ground. Roses always make better plants if supplied in this way, because their roots hate being restricted in the confined space of a container. Nowadays the majority of our planting is done using containerized plants. Apart from the convenience, you can see what you are buying. *Callicarpa bodinieri* var. *giraldii* may not inspire you to buy it solely on its name, but when you see it for sale, covered in its luminous purple-violet berries in late autumn and winter, you are hooked and must buy it!

Do try to avoid buying one of this and one of that on your frequent forays to the garden centre, but rather purchase plants in quantities of three or five. This prevents the garden looking spotty, and groups of plants do give the border an established look.

By now, most of the bulbs should have been planted to give a display in the spring, but ideally tulips should not go in until the end of November or early December: if planted before this, the leaves appear just after Christmas and their soft tips can be damaged by frost, leaving them unsightly when they are in flower. Make sure you remember to plant all bulbs at an angle of 45 degrees, having previously dipped them in methylated spirits. If planted straight up and we have a wet winter, the rain percolates down through the soil into the centre of the bulb and rots it; by putting bulbs in at an angle, the rain runs down the side of the bulb and does no damage. The purpose of the meths is that the smell of it keeps rodents from eating the bulb, and it protects the bulb from fungal attack.

Now follows a list of plants that should be in your garden in the winter to give you colour either by flower or by stems and bark, and possibly a few berries and fruits hanging on from the autumn.

Plants that provide coloured stems or bark include Cornus, Betula and Rubus. Two beautiful winter-flowering clematis are *C. cirrhosa* and *C. armandii*. Another useful climber at this time of the year is *Jasminum nudiflorum*, which is covered for weeks and weeks with delightful, golden yellow star-shaped flowers. Many grasses provide interest not only in their fading plumes but also in their decorative foliage.

Fruits and berries will often still be there from the autumn: this is true of the crab apples, particularly the variety Golden Hornet, the Sorbus (mountain ash) family, and *Arbutus x andrachnoides*, which will have pearly, luminous flowers, but at the same time will carry pendulous strawberry-like fruits both in shape and colour. It gives additional value in that it has peeling, russet-coloured bark.

The hollies (Ilex) provide a wide range of coloured leaves and berries. Conifers – both large- and small-growing varieties – provide winter interest. *Crytomeria japonica* is evergreen, but its green foliage turns to a warm brown in the winter, and then back to green in the spring; and *Juniperous squamata* (Blue Star) has startling blue foliage, highlighted even more on a frosty morning.

Winter-flowering shrubs should include *Garrya elliptica*, with its pendulous grey-green catkins; *Skimmia reevesiana* 'Rubella', with its decorative flower trusses; and the winter-flowering heathers (*Erica carnea*), which come in a wide range of colours and remain in flower for many weeks. A very underrated group of shrubs are the dwarfish *sarcococcas* with wavy-edged, dark green, small evergreen leaves; but it is their tiny, very fragrant flowers that are one of the highlights of the winter garden, particularly if planted adjacent to a well-used door or a ground-floor window that may be opened on a bright winter's morning.

Daphne mezereum has already been mentioned, and another daphne well worth finding a space for is *D. odora* 'Aureo-marginata'. As its name implies, it is very fragrant. There are two wonderful specimens planted each side of the entrance to the conservatory in Barbara Hepworth's garden in St Ives, Cornwall.

Eleagnus and Euonymus are important residents in the winter by nature of their diverse foliage, both green and variegated, and some also produce flowers, although they tend to be insignificant. The evergreen Hederas (ivies) can be used as either climbers or as ground coverers, particularly in shady places.

Finally, *Ribes laurifolium* should get a mention: it is an evergreen, spreading shrub with very leathery evergreen leaves, and pendant yellow-green flowers.

SPRING

In March, April and May, spring is upon us every-where; flowers are appearing on trees, shrubs, herbaceous plants and bulbs. The grass is growing – but so too are the weeds! Things seem to be happening overnight, and they are. The weather can be very variable, sunny one moment, cold the next, especially if the winds are northerly or easterly.

The Easter holiday dates vary between March and April, but this is when the gardening year starts, according to the majority of the population. With so much happening and so much to do all at once, the most important thing is not to panic. You can't do it all at once, so quietly walk round the garden and make a list of what there is to do. Then sit down with a drink and make a revised list of the jobs in their priority. As you work down the list, tackle each job properly, don't rush it: if you do, it won't be long before it needs doing again. As each task is completed, tick it off on the list. To see the list shrinking will give you a great feeling of satisfaction. If for some reason the job you want to do next is going to be difficult because of adverse weather conditions, switch to the next one – though make sure you return to the undone task before it's too late!

Springtime Tasks

It may be wise to tackle pruning first. Plants such as *Caryopteris*, *Perovskia*, *Ceanothus* 'Gloire de Versaille', *Spiraea japonica*, hardy fuchsias and the late-flowering clematis such as *C. 'Jackmanii'* and the group of clematis 'Viticella', all need pruning hard back now, as they flower on the new wood they produce during the spring and early summer. The early-flowering shrubs such as forsythia, *Ribes* (flowering currant) and *Viburnum fragrans*, whose flowers are finished or past their best, need the stems that have flowered to be removed to encourage new growth to form, because this will become the flowering wood for the following year.

In the herbaceous border, plants are making rapid growth, and it is better to stake them at this stage rather than leave it too late. Plants that make in excess of 3ft (90cm) of growth in a season, particularly in an exposed position, should be staked

now. Prunings of corylus (hazel) make excellent natural support; bamboo canes can be used, but they tend to give a harsh feel to the borders. Bundles of hazel can often be found in garden centres, farm shops and farmers' markets.

After staking would be a good time to apply a quick-acting fertilizer such as Growmore, combined with a dressing of chicken pellet manure, both at the rate of a handful per square yard or metre. Having staked and fed the bed, it will be covered in your footprints, so now is the time to obliterate them with a hoe, which at the same time will kill off any emerging weed seedlings.

Planting

Apart from adding plants that you see and like at the garden centre, now is the time to put in some of the unusual summer and autumn bulbs that are seldom seen in our gardens. We tend only to think of spring-flowering bulbs. Alstroemeria must always be purchased as pot-grown, as they have a very fragile root system, but once established are easy to cultivate. Crocosmia, both short and tall varieties, Galtonia, lilies, Nerines, Zephyranthes, Sparaxis and Tigridia, to mention only a few, flower in July and August. Like the spring bulbs, they do not have to have a specific planting space of their own, but bloom by emerging through other plants' foliage.

While we are busy planting the summer bulbs, those that were planted in the previous autumn have either finished flowering or are coming to their end. The fading flower heads should be removed, unless you want them to form seed and thereby naturalize, such as snowdrops and aconites. The foliage of the bulbs should be watered with a solution of a seaweed-based fertilizer such as Maxicrop or Seagold, at the rate of one tablespoonful to a gallon of water, to which has been added five or six drops of washing-up liquid and stirred in. The purpose of this is that the washing-up liquid makes the solution stick to the leaves so it cannot be washed off by showers of rain. The solution passes down through the foliage and feeds the bulb. Repeat this in two weeks' time, and two weeks after that the foliage can be cut down to ground level as the bulb will then be fully fed, ready for next year's flowering.

Keep lawns mown on a regular basis throughout the summer.

Places can be found in the borders for pyramids, up which you can grow sweet peas, melons and gourds. Try incorporating vegetable plants into a mixed flower and shrub border, especially if space is at a premium. Salad crops can go in the front of such a scheme. Using pyramids can give additional interest to what otherwise would be a flat area. One pot of young sweet-pea plants positioned in the centre of the structure will provide you with a mass of colour, perfume and flowers to pick. Seven to ten days after planting the sweet peas, pinch the growing tips out, and soon they will be growing up the structure. The more you pick the flowers, the more will come. Runner beans, gourds and melons can be sown as seed straight into the open ground at the base of the support, or can be purchased as young plants.

Spring is not too late to scarify, aerate and apply an application of 'weed and feed' to the lawn. If you do this, remember not to put the first two grass clippings on to the compost heap, as they may contain residues of the weed killer.

Seed sowing should begin in earnest. Only recently have annual flower seeds come back into fashion. They are such good value, and if regularly de-headed they will go on flowering profusely right throughout the season. There are annuals suitable for any position in the garden, sun or shade, dry or damp.

The vegetable garden – hopefully cultivated and free of weeds – should be ready to receive seeds of beans, peas and salad crops, and onion and shallot sets. If you have a greenhouse or cold frame, you should have been able to sow seed earlier, which in turn will have led to the production of young plants; if these are hardened off and planted out, they will give the feeling that the vegetable garden has always been producing crops. Like the ornamental part of the garden, the vegetable garden should be fed on a regular basis, and have humus worked in whenever possible.

SUMMER

No sooner has spring started, then suddenly it's all over and we are into summer.

Summer is probably the busiest of all the seasons. The early part of the summer season is a great time for both seed sowing and planting, to provide a succession of things to eat and blooms to cut.

There is so much to do, with the foliage still remaining of the late flowering bulbs and the pruning of the late flowering spring shrubs. After adverse weather conditions it might not be possible to apply dressing and treatment to the lawn before you start to think of summer tasks to be undertaken. However, you must not think that the whole of the summer is a series of never-ending tasks, because with careful planning it shouldn't be. There should be time to enjoy your garden, especially with the days getting longer. With the advent of climate change we should get used to enjoying the garden more, to sitting in it, eating in it or, if not time for this, at least sitting and enjoying a drink in it.

Time should be allocated to visiting gardens belonging to family and friends, to see what they are up to, particularly if, like you, they garden on clay. Or visit the many gardens open under the National Gardens Scheme (buy the 'yellow book' published annually each spring), especially those on clay; the owners of these gardens are very approachable, and they are quite willing to give advice, and to tell you of their problems, as well as their successes, in getting the garden to look as it does now.

Holidays will also intrude into this season, and preparations must be made well in advance of going away so that the garden doesn't look a mess on your return.

Summer Tasks

Before you rush into seed sowing and planting, did you de-head the last of the late spring flowering bulbs, and foliar feed their foliage? If not, provided the foliage has not started to go yellow at the tips, there is still time to do this – maybe only once, but this is better than not doing it at all, and you will see benefits of this next spring. Late flowering spring shrubs such as lilacs, cytisus (brooms) and ceanothus should at least have their dead flowers removed, as you don't want them to waste energy in producing seed that you don't want. Last year's growth can be reduced by one third to keep the shrubs under control where required.

Probably the most important job you can do is to continue to de-head. It is also very therapeutic. De-heading is not always a question of removing the faded flowers. For instance, Canterbury bells should have the faded flowers rubbed off, not cut. Do wear a pair of gloves when you do this, otherwise your fingers will be covered in tiny prickles. Having rubbed off the flowers, new flower buds will soon appear to take their place. Plants such as annuals, and many herbaceous plants and dahlias, should have not just their faded flowers cut off, but should be cut back to a healthy growth or shoot. If you just remove the flowers, the stems that were supporting the flowers will continue to lengthen, making the plants look unsightly. If a job is worth doing, it's worth doing well.

It is never too late to scarify, aerate and feed the lawn, although if you hit a dry spell it may be necessary after applying the feed to water the lawn thoroughly in the cool of the evening, to prevent scorching. After scarifying, bald patches may appear, but seed can be sown in these patches, and will germinate in a few days in these warm conditions. Again, water carefully if no natural rainfall is forecast.

Throughout the summer, keep the lawns mown on a regular basis – and be prepared to adjust the height of the cutting blades. So many gardeners cut at the same height whatever the weather. If you hit a dry spell, a longer length will keep the roots cool, thus not putting too much stress on growth.

Finally, throughout the summer season remember to continue to foliar feed every two weeks. It is also essential that you keep an eye out for the emergence of pests and diseases, and spray accordingly.

Sowing and Growing

Vegetable seed sowing should be in full swing to provide you with a continuous supply of both fresh salad crops and vegetables. The golden rule with seed sowing is to sow a little on a regular basis, rather than the whole packet all at once. Who wants 200 lettuce plants all ready to be eaten at the same time! Once the seed packet has been opened and the amount taken out that you require, the packet should be resealed by wrapping it in either clingfilm or foil, which will keep the seed fresh and viable until next time you want to use it. If you have started late with your seed sowing, it may be advisable to purchase young vegetable and salad plants from your local nursery or garden centre while the seed gets going.

Bedding plants will be for sale everywhere, even on garage forecourts, but resist the temptation to purchase them until you are sure that all risk of frost has passed. Don't necessarily plant the same varieties that you did the previous year, just because they did well, but ring the changes. The important thing with bedding plants is to plant generous quantities of each variety you select. So often one sees twelve planted where really twenty or thirty should have gone in. You don't want to see bare earth between the plants: what you want to see is a carpet of foliage and flowers. Not only does this look good, but their closeness ensures that the soil beneath keeps cool, thus helping moisture retention, and because no light can penetrate, weed seedlings do not develop. Always give the trays or pots a thorough watering the night before you intend to plant them, and water the position in which they are to go. This also applies to containerized shrubs or roses, and if you plant in the

Onorpordum arabacium *(Scotch thistle).*

early morning or evening, this gets them off to a good start.

In the flower garden the season starts with paeonies and *Iris germanica.* So much breeding and hybridizing has been going on in the last few years that there is now a much larger selection to choose from. But *Iris* 'Jane Phillips' must still come very high on any list of selected varieties, for its fabulous Mediterranean blue colour and its outstanding fragrance. Of the paeonies, again another old variety, *P. festiva* 'Maxima' – a double-frilled flower, pure white in colour with the occasional flecks of red at its base – is a lovely variety to grow. It is usually recommended to plant in groups of three or five, but in the case of paeonies, a single plant is sufficient to give the display required. Paeonies, particularly the doubled-flowered varieties, can hang their heads after a summer shower, but soon dry out and return, unspoiled, to their original position. Nip the blooms off as they fade but retain as much of their foliage as possible, as many varieties produce won-

derful autumn tints. Neither paeonies nor iris produce a second flowering in the same season.

Hemerocallis is another suitable plant for the clay garden in summer; its common name is the day lily, because each flower lasts only a day. However, as there are many buds on each stem, you will have a continual display. Like the paeonies and iris, some are scented, and continual breeding programmes are widening the colour range. Four of the best newer varieties are 'Cranberry Baby' (red), 'Indian Chief' (tawny orange brown), 'Pandora's Box' (creamy yellow with a red throat) and 'White Temptation'.

If you want perfume in the garden, then the many forms of *Phlox paniculata* will provide it from late July well into the autumn. Once the main flower at the top of the stem has finished, remove it, and all the way up the stem side flowers will emerge, not as spectacular as the first one, but providing a back-up display. 'David' is a lovely, white, scented variety; 'Laura' is purple and heavily scented; and 'Nicky' is also purple and scented.

Two plants that are majestic in the summer border when in flower are *Crambe cordifolia*, which literally carries hundreds of tiny, white, star-shaped flowers, and *Macleaya macrocarpa*, the plume poppy, particularly the variety 'coral plume'. Once flowering has finished, they leave big gaps in the border because they are not repeat flowerers. Therefore plant the tall *Artemisia lactiflora* and *Eupatorium rugosum* 'Chocolate' in front of them to take over and replace the height that you had planned. The tall-growing Thalictrums with their lime green or delicate mauve flowers, depending on the variety selected, look lovely when inter-planted through the Artemisia and Eupatorium, giving a feeling of lightness to the scheme. For architectural and staggering effect, use isolated specimens of Onorpordum in beds and borders.

The astrantias have really come into their own, with the vast selection of colours, but *Astrantia major*, which has greenish-pink flowers, is not only lovely in itself, but is so good at creating striking plant associations. As soon as the first flowers fade, cut it hard back, including the foliage, and a second, and even a third display will follow. Astrantias are one of the first plants to show signs of distress if the soil dries out through lack of moisture, so as soon as this happens, give each individual plant a generous can of water.

Very much a highlight of any summer border are the eryngiums, the sea hollies, which usually have electric blue flowers surrounded by architectural foliage, sometimes marbled. They are made even more wonderful if they have carpets of pink herbaceous geraniums, or are planted in association with pink penstemons such as *P.* 'Hewell pink bedder' or *P.* 'Hidcote pink'. To be very daring, plant *P.* 'Garnet' with them; it has scarlet tubular flowers over a very long period into a mild winter. Penstemons, unlike most herbaceous plants, should only be lightly trimmed in the autumn, the main pruning being carried out in the spring.

Other occupants of the summer border could be selected from forms of *Phygelius*, *Physostegia*, *Anemone japonica*, *A. hupensis*, *Campanula lactiflora* and Echinacea. Yet another choice here could be *Verbena bonariensis*, which once planted will cast its seed all ways, but never becomes a nuisance. Spindly in growth, it seems to bring a border together, popping up in the most unexpected places.

Holiday Hints

Prior to going away for your summer holiday, do everything you can to help the plants, whether they are decorative or edible, to continue to be at their best for the rest of the season, but also so that on your return you have a wealth of newly opened flowers and things to eat. This entails removing the flowers that are just going over, but also those that will be past their best on your return. Pick all the flowers on the sweet peas, even those just bursting, likewise runner beans, French beans and courgettes. The beans could go into the freezer; similarly the herbs can be cropped and frozen. Ensure the foliage of the herbs is dry before putting them in polythene bags, otherwise they will rot. This will make you feel that all your efforts have been worthwhile.

If the beds and borders were mulched in the spring there will be sufficient moisture under the surface to support plant growth while you are away. However, if there is not a ban on using hosepipes, a thorough watering would be beneficial. Hopefully a kindly neighbour will come to your aid by watering

SUMMER SHRUBS FOR THE CLAY GARDEN

Towards the end of summer, shrubs that were pruned in the spring when their flowering had finished will show some flowers, not as profuse as the first display, but well worth a place. *Choisya ternata* (Mexican orange blossom) is an example. Other shrubs that should be in the summer garden include:

- *Escallonias*
- Hydrangeas, both mophead and lacecap varieties
- *Holodiscus discolor* (seldom seen, but has wonderful pendant creamy flowers and good autumn colour)
- *Kolkwitiza amabilis* (the beauty bush)
- *Abelia grandiflora* or its varieties – never out of flower from July until the first frost
- Buddleias, especially the grey foliage varieties, which attract butterflies
- Perovskias, with their staggering blue sprays and cut-leafed aromatic foliage
- Sambucus (elders) – the black- and golden-leaved varieties
- The much maligned privets (*Ligustrums*), if allowed to grow without being clipped, form wonderful free-flowing bushes that are semi-evergreen and give a touch of lightness to a planting scheme – they are also very useful to have as a regular dot plant to unite a scheme in a long border.

your containerized pots and baskets, and if you have a greenhouse, this as well. If no neighbour is about, you can do things to mitigate any damage. Move the containers and baskets into the shadiest part of the garden. If the containers are made of wood, they can have furniture castors fitted to their base, thus making it easy to move them about. Garden centres and DIY stores sell pot trolleys that fit under the pots to help move them. After all, the last thing you want to do is to strain your back before going away. Once moved into their temporary position, give all the containers a thorough soaking. If the containers were lined with sodden

Rhus typhina.

newspaper prior to planting, this will also help to keep the moisture levels up. If possible, stand the containers in dishes full of water, as this will help to keep the humidity down.

Looking to the Future

All the time we should not only be busy with maintaining what we have got, but we also have to think about what we want to have next year. So seed-sowing of wallflowers, Canterbury bells and sweet williams in the open ground should be carried out either in July or August; when big enough to handle they should then be transplanted into nursery rows. Shortly afterwards pinch out their tips to make them into bushy plants. They will finally be ready for planting out into their permanent positions in September or October.

AUTUMN

Autumn is possibly the loveliest of the four seasons. The whole landscape changes as the summer's greens start to look tired. Magically, it turns into the most dazzling shades of crimson, red, orange, apricot, lemon and yellow. Each autumn is different, the colours being so dependent on what the summer has been like; thus a wet summer intensifies the colour and lets foliage remain on the trees and shrubs longer, whereas a dry summer stops the plants taking up the sugar that helps to create the colour and intensity of autumn leaves.

Autumn Plants

As already mentioned elsewhere in the book, when purchasing plants to go in the garden, what should be very high on the list of considerations is not only flower value, the possibility of it bearing fruits or berries, and the value of its bark or stems, but also its potential to produce autumn colour. There is a great deal to be said for going to the garden centre or nursery and selecting plants bearing their autumnal colours in late September to mid-November, as quite often plants are raised from seed and their colouring can vary enormously.

In addition, seeing plants established impresses their colours on our minds. *Liquidambar styraciflua* is a classic example: it is so variable, and to purchase it at other times is a great mistake, because it will always be a disappointing colour.

Other more unusual shrubs to have in the garden include *Cotinus coggyria* 'Flame' or the maples (Acers), which do well both as trees and shrubs. Having a wide colour range in their autumnal display, many have interesting bark as well. *Euonymus europaeus* and its many varieties do splendidly on clay, as does *E. hamiltonianus* 'Red Elf'.

Not only does the Cornus family (dogwoods) have very attractive bark in the winter, but their foliage does colour up well in the autumn, too – *C. kesselringii* being one of the best. The aronias and vacciniums do surprisingly well on clay soil, provided they are given an annual mulch of well-rotted humus combined with a fertilizer feed each spring. They are very under-rated shrubs, which is surprising considering their fabulous autumn colour. *V. angustifolium* and *V. parvifolium* are the best of the vacciniums, and *Aronia arbutifolia* and *A. melanocarpa* are the best of the aronias.

Autumn Tasks

It is so important to get the garden tidied up before Christmas. Failure to do this, combined with a wet January and February, means you will have a difficult task ahead before the arrival of Easter.

CHAPTER 14

Climate Change

Climate change has been very much in the news over the last few years and, as gardeners, we need to think about how it will affect the way we garden and what we can do to adapt to it. This should be on every gardener's mind, even if we prefer not to think about it!

Whether we like it or not, climate change is happening all around us, and we have to accept it as a definite fact. The purpose of this chapter is to be very positive, not negative – which is all too easy when contemplating the unknown. Yes, it may mean that in a few years' time some of the plants that are so familiar in our gardens today may be unable to cope with the change in growing conditions. However, the plus point is that some of the plants we have seen on our holidays abroad, and longed to grow here, will become permanent residents in our beds and borders.

Within a short space of time, the appearance of our gardens could change dramatically. Exciting, isn't it?

CONSERVING WATER

The key to coping with this dramatic change is water and its conservation. One important way of helping to conserve water is by not allowing weeds to grow and flourish, because while they are doing this, they are using water.

We should maximize on saving the amount of water that comes off our roofs by increasing the number of down-pipes that come from the gutters. Each down-pipe should feed into one or more

water butts. Provided that two or three water butts are set at different levels from each other, they should, with the right connections, feed from the tallest to the lowest. It is quite possible that one day it will become mandatory that when builders build new houses they will have to install in the foundations a water storage tank complete with a pump for garden use.

MULCHING

With the advent of climate change, mulching will become an essential part of any garden maintenance programme. As soon as the winter rains have finished in February or March, the moisture must be retained in the soil as long as possible by applying an annual surface mulch some 2 to 3in (5 to 8cm) deep all over the surface of the soil, whether it is planted or not.

The mulch can be spent mushroom compost from local mushroom farms, spent hops from local breweries, well-rotted garden compost, well-rotted farmyard manure, bark, and any other organic material. The spent mushroom compost and the spent hops have two advantages over every other type of mulch: they are very light to handle, making them easy to wheel to any part of the garden that needs mulching. The nature of their processing causes the heat generated to kill off any weed seeds, which is not the case with the garden and farmyard materials.

Clay soil is notorious in that it does not readily retain moisture, but with one or two dressings of Claybreaker and regular mulching, its moisture retention should soon improve. At planting time always work in as much mulching material both to the planting position and the surrounding area.

Geraniums love dry conditions.

FERTILIZERS AND FOLIAR FEED

On clay soil, don't think that having planted correctly, that's it: on the contrary, you must follow it up with an annual spring mulch and, if possible, with applications of foliar feed as well. If there is no sign of any mulch remaining on the soil surface in the autumn, then another application after the first autumnal rains would be most beneficial. To further improve the soil condition as far as plant growth is concerned, apply a twice yearly dressing of sterilized fish, blood and bone, and Gromore in October and March – a handful per square metre.

The foliar feed should be of a seaweed-based fertilizer such as Seagold, which is high in trace elements that are essential to plant growth. At present we only foliar feed during May, June and July, but once we know climate change has finally arrived, we can extend the feeding time from April to September at fortnightly intervals. We may also find that we have to resort to old-fashioned methods, such as tying a stocking filled with organic manure to the bottom of every downpipe: the rainwater passing through it before entering the water butt thereby provides us with a constant supply of liquid feed.

PLANTS AND CLIMATE CHANGE

Will plants be able to adapt to climate change? Some will, and some won't. Plants with shallow roots will find it much harder to survive than those with deep and thong-like roots. These will include silver birch and rhododendron, both of which have very shallow, congested root systems. Those with deep roots, such as the rose and acanthus, will happily survive.

Unfortunately groundcover plants such as the Vinca family (periwinkle), and the Pulmonaria (lungwort) and Lamium (ornamental nettle) families will be among the first to disappear from our gardens. We will have to replace these with deep-rooting perennials in greater numbers so they grow into each other; then their dense leaf cover will shade the ground, keeping it cool and weed-free, and conserving the moisture at the same time. Herbaceous plants that show signs of stress should be cut down to ground level, and given a can or

Salvia officinalis *'Purpurea' – purple sage.*

cans of water – not all at once, but applied gradually over a couple of hours. Very quickly new, dense foliage followed by flowers will appear.

As a nation we are so frightened of cutting back that we let our lupins, oriental poppies and delphiniums flower once, and then think that's that! We fail to realize that if they are given the chop, they will nevertheless come back and start the process all over again. In Chapter 7 and Chapter 13 you will find detailed explanations on the cutting back of herbaceous plants when flowering has finished (*see* pages 50 and 94-5).

The whole object of a flowering plant's life is to produce flowers, but if it is allowed to produce seed, no more flowers will come. Seeds are scattered by wind, or sown by hand, or the plants self-seed – but we have to prevent this happening if we want these plants to continue. Where there are shrubby plants in the herbaceous border, such as penstemons, these cannot be cut to ground level and must be continually deadheaded.

Bedding plants such as the winter pansies, polyanthus and wallflowers might still be seen, but some of our summer ones will go. The geraniums and gazanias will be fine, and some of the more exotic bedding plants will replace those that cannot cope with the newer growing conditions.

However, we have to be careful that we don't all jump on the same bandwagon. In fact people are already doing this by planting a cordyline and two or three shrubs, and then covering the ground with shingle – and they think this is the answer to climate change. This is certainly *not* the right approach: it's just the easy way out. If we all did this our gardens would become boring and totally unsuited to our beautiful English landscape and our way of gardening, which is the envy of the world. We must retain this 'look' for as long as we can, albeit with some changes along the way.

On a positive note, some of the plants we have seen on our holidays abroad, and which we have been longing to grow, may now come within our reach. If we could incorporate some of these in our existing schemes, that would be a step in the right direction. Some of the plants we should be able to grow in the next few years include:

- Acacia
- Tibouchiana
- Leptospermums
- Myrtus
- Pittosporums
- Datura
- Abutilons
- Oleanders
- Draceana
- Protea
- Medinella
- Prostranthus
- Callistemons

Some of these already grow in the milder climes of Cornwall and the west coast of Scotland and in some sheltered gardens throughout the country, but these are just a very few of the possibilities. Oranges, lemons and grapefruit will become the norm. Succulents will become an integral part of planting schemes – although some, such as aloes, may require protection or covers to protect them from too much rain rotting their centres.

HERBS

Of all the plants, herbs are going to revel in climate change, and because their growth will be vigorous they must be harvested on a regular basis. Surplus cut herbs can be kept in the freezer in polythene bags. If not harvested regularly, herbs will become long, lanky and tired. In addition, because of the excessive growth, it is vital that a regular liquid feeding programme is carried out. Basil and tarragon, which are currently not the easiest to grow, will almost become weeds, and will need to be grown in containers.

LAWNS

It may happen that conventional lawns will become a thing of the past, but this will be a gradual process. For the moment, provided our lawns are given the tender loving care they need (as outlined in Chapter 4), they will survive. It is always amazing that when we have experienced a period of drought and our lawns have gone brown, how soon they recover after the first rains of autumn. So be sure to aerate and scarify lawns more often, followed by a weed and feed: look after them in adverse conditions and they would survive even longer before turning brown. A dressing of spent mushroom compost applied 1in (3cm) thick every spring would also preclude the possibility of browning.

Lawns sown with New Zealand fescue grass seed will become more common than they are now, because they survive drought better than any other grass: in even the driest conditions, their foliage only becomes tinged with a tint of red. Fragrant lawns of thyme, peppermint and chamomile – again, plants that survive the driest conditions in Greece and Turkey – will come into their own, especially once people realize that on a hot day they don't have to mow!

If you try to maintain a conventional lawn, you may have to adapt to the concept of not cutting the grass too short, as by leaving the grass blades longer they keep the grass roots shaded and therefore cooler. Even in our present conditions, cutting too short puts enormous pressure on the roots to provide new growth.

DESIGN FEATURES

Even existing gardens may have to have some parts redesigned. For example, sloping beds that at one time were constructed to get rid of surplus moisture, may now have to be levelled to retain it.

However, those with new gardens can of course start with a blank canvas, and in this case a number of design features need to be considered.

Shade

Certainly as temperatures rise, shade will become a top priority, both for us and the existing planting. The incorporation of trees will help in this, and varieties from the robinia family, catalpas and paulownias will both do this and provide a new feel to the garden. *Gleditschia* 'Sunburst' would be a lovely addition, and who could not be impressed when any of the Paulownia species, with their enormous leaves and their blue foxglove-shaped flowers are out?

For additional shade we may have to turn to man-made structures to help us out, such as more umbrellas placed throughout the garden – but remember they are to complement the planting, not compete with it, so try to use plain colours only. Awnings coming out from various parts of the house will be useful, but again, keep to neutral colours, not stripes and patterns.

Water Features

If we can sit beneath the shade of a tree or umbrella and hear the sound of running water, no matter how small, it will make us feel cool. A wall fountain using recycled water will be well worth its cost. If there is room for it, there is no reason why a pond cannot be introduced into the design of your garden; it will undoubtedly provide a very attractive feature in a warmer climate. However, its depth and size must relate to the safety factor, not only of your own children, if you have any, but any potential young visitors as well. To see a pond for the very first time is an invitation to get as near to it as you possibly can, and this is when potentially it becomes a serious hazard. It can have a fence all round it, but this destroys its beauty, even if the fence can be camouflaged by greenery – but this is still not always the answer, as you probably want to look across the pond to the view beyond.

Taking the above into consideration and you still want a pond, the most important design feature must be how you line the excavated area to hold the

Preformed pond shapes.

water. More than any other soil, clay expands and contracts according to weather temperature, so what you line the pond with must be able to react to this constant change. Therefore concrete or similar would not be suitable, but instead a rubber butyl liner should be used; these are expensive to purchase, but they are the only practical solution in the long run. If you can obtain some old carpet material and place it between the wall of soil and the butyl, this will prevent any sharp stones or flints puncturing the liner; this is particularly important below the base of the liner, where the maximum weight and pressure will be exerted.

Do site the pond in as open a position as possible, because if there is overhanging foliage, leaves from the trees and shrubs will fall into the water and decay.

A pond is a great way of introducing wildlife into the garden. Frogs and toads will be the first occupants, quickly followed by numerous species of birds that come to drink and bathe. Dragonflies and butterflies will skim across its surface or come to rest on the leaves of the waterlilies if you have planted some.

Container Gardening

We may have to reduce the number of containers we have: far better to do a few superbly, than have a lot struggling. Thus hanging baskets may become

Left: Ponds can be designed to blend in with the surrounding planting.

Below: Waterlilies always add charm to a garden pond.

Symphytum officinalis aureum – *comfrey.*

a thing of the past, or at least the summer ones, because of the need for daily watering. Maybe those planted for winter/spring display will survive, as there should be adequate water available then to keep them going.

Terracotta pots are helped by being immersed in water before they are planted, and then the base and sides need to be lined with sodden newspaper. It must be at least 1in (3cm) below the rim of the pot and covered by compost so that the sun's rays do not strike the paper and dry it out. By doing this you will reduce the amount of water required.

CONCLUSION

This is as far as we can go at the moment, but this should make you feel easier about progressing climate change. You will have lots to learn, and certainly you will make mistakes. It may be advantageous to go out and buy a notebook, call it *Climate Change*, and record anything you notice of significance. It will be invaluable and useful as time passes. Above all, don't be fearful of climate change. Enjoy the challenges that it offers, and sometimes sit in the shade of your newly planted trees and enjoy your garden.

Index